THE SECRET LIVES
OF STONE CIRCLES

Megaliths, Ley Lines, and Energy Vortices

D.R. T STEPHENS

S.D.N Publishing

CONTENTS

GENERAL DISCLAIMER

This book is intended to provide general information to the reader on the topics covered. The author and publisher have made every effort to ensure that the information herein is accurate and up-to-date at the time of publication. However, they do not warrant or guarantee the accuracy, completeness, adequacy, or currency of the information contained in this book. The author and publisher expressly disclaim any liability or responsibility for any errors or omissions in the content herein.

The information, guidance, advice, tips, and suggestions provided in this book are not intended to replace professional advice or consultation. Readers are strongly encouraged to consult with an appropriate professional for specific advice tailored to their situation before making any decisions or taking any actions based on the content of this book.

The views and opinions expressed in this book are those of the author and do not necessarily reflect the official policy or position of any other agency, organization, employer or company.

The author and publisher are not responsible for any actions taken or not taken by the reader based on the information, advice, or suggestions provided in this book. The reader is solely responsible for their actions and the consequences thereof.

This book is not intended to be a source of legal, business, medical or psychological advice, and readers are cautioned to seek the services of a competent professional in these or other areas of expertise.

All product names, logos, and brands are property of their respective owners. All company, product and service names used in this book are for identification purposes only. Use of these names, logos, and brands does not imply endorsement.

Readers of this book are advised to do their own due diligence when it comes to making decisions and all information, products, services and advice that have been provided should be independently verified by your own qualified professionals.

By reading this book, you agree that the author and publisher are not responsible for your success or failure resulting from any information presented in this book.

CHAPTER 1: INTRODUCTION TO STONE CIRCLES

Section 1.1: Definition and Historical Context

Stone circles, a term that brings to mind ancient landscapes and bygone civilizations, are essentially concentric arrangements of stones, typically large and upright, in a circular fashion. But these simple configurations offer much more than what meets the eye. The stone circles that we discuss are megalithic structures, the term "megalith" originating from the ancient Greek words 'megas,' meaning 'big,' and 'lithos,' meaning 'stone.'

The historical context of stone circles is indeed a vast tapestry interwoven with threads of archaeology, anthropology, folklore, and even spirituality. The tradition of erecting stone circles dates back to prehistoric times, somewhere between 3000 BCE to 1500 BCE in regions such as Europe. The most famous among them, Stonehenge in the United Kingdom, dates back to around 3000 BCE and has been a subject of extensive archaeological research.

But why did ancient humans invest significant time and labor in constructing these circles? While definitive answers are elusive, researchers have advanced various theories. Some see stone circles as ceremonial or religious sites, places where communities would gather for rites and rituals. Others consider these stone arrangements as early astronomical tools used for marking solar, lunar, or stellar events. Still, others think of them as territorial markers or gathering places for social activities.

Stone circles were not built in isolation. They are often part of a larger complex of structures, including burial mounds and menhirs (single-standing stones), which provide vital clues about the purpose and usage of these circles. They are also found in diverse geological settings, from the rocky terrains of Scotland to the sandy soils of the African Savannah, indicating a practice that transcended regional cultures.

It's important to note that the practice of erecting stone circles was not confined to any one part of the world. While Europe is abundant with such formations, especially in areas like the British Isles, stone circles are also found in other continents. For example, the Senegambian stone circles in West Africa offer compelling evidence that this practice was more widespread than initially thought. The range of these circles, both geographically and culturally, has implications for how we understand human civilizations and their interactions with the natural world.

Various cultural narratives have developed around stone circles over the centuries. These circles have been imbued with mystical properties in folklore, and they continue to fascinate the public and researchers alike. Their mystical allure often takes shape in modern spiritual practices, New Age beliefs, and even literature and art. This public interest, in turn, contributes to their preservation as historical and cultural landmarks.

Additionally, advances in technologies such as LIDAR (Light Detection and Ranging) and material analysis have paved the way for more nuanced understandings of these ancient structures. Archaeologists and historians now have more tools at their disposal to unravel the secrets that these stone circles hold.

In summary, stone circles are not merely archaic configurations of large stones. They are complex structures that offer glimpses into the social, religious, and possibly astronomical aspects of the communities that built them. Although much has been discovered about these fascinating structures, they continue to pose questions that prompt researchers to dig deeper, both literally and metaphorically. With every layer that is uncovered, we come closer to understanding our ancestors' lives and, by extension, our own human story.

SECTION 1.2: GEOGRAPHICAL DISTRIBUTION

While stone circles hold a special fascination for many, it's vital to realize that these enigmatic structures are not confined to any one part of the world. Rather, they are scattered across various geographical terrains, each site reflecting unique cultural, historical, and environmental conditions. This section aims to provide an overview of the geographical distribution of stone circles, highlighting regions where these formations are prominently found.

Europe: A Rich Tapestry of Stone Circles

The British Isles are often considered a hub for stone circles, with famous examples like Stonehenge in England and the Ring of Brodgar in Scotland. However, these are just the tip of the iceberg. Wales, Ireland, and even parts of mainland Europe, such as Scandinavia, have their fair share of these ancient structures. For instance, the Carnac stones in Brittany, France, are a significant megalithic site. The cold, windswept Orkney Islands in Scotland are another treasure trove, featuring several lesser-known but equally fascinating stone circles.

Africa: Beyond the Sahara

Stone circles in Africa are less discussed but equally captivating. The Senegambian stone circles, located primarily in Gambia and Senegal, are notable examples. These sites are especially intriguing because of their diversity in terms of size, design, and the stones used. Furthermore, some circles have been found in the Ethiopian highlands, providing a tantalizing hint at a broader prehistoric tradition on the continent.

Asia and the Middle East: An Untapped Wealth

Asia, too, holds its share of mysteries with ancient stone arrangements. In India, the states of Karnataka and Maharashtra boast menhirs and megalithic circles that date back to prehistoric times. Meanwhile, in the Middle East, Jordan's "Big Circles" are large stone structures that have intrigued archaeologists for years. However, due to geopolitical reasons and other constraints, some of these sites have not been as thoroughly researched as their European counterparts.

Americas: From the North to the South

Moving westward to the Americas, one encounters a variety of stone circles, though they are often not megalithic in the same way as those in Europe or Africa. Medicine wheels in North America, particularly in areas like Wyoming and Alberta, are ritualistic stone arrangements made by indigenous peoples. In South America, the Amazon Stonehenge, or "Regalito," in Brazil is an example of stone circles that may have served as an astronomical calendar.

Oceania: The Pacific Islands

Though fewer in number, stone circles do exist in the Pacific region. Tonga's Haʻamonga ʻa Maui and the stone money banks in Yap, Micronesia, are among the examples. While not "circles" in the strictest sense, these stone arrangements hold cultural and possibly ritualistic significance for local populations.

The geographical distribution of stone circles is a testament to the universality of human curiosity and reverence for the natural world. Whether made for ritualistic, astronomical, or yet-unknown reasons, these ancient stone formations are found in virtually every corner of the globe. This widespread distribution invites questions about possible cultural exchanges in antiquity, or perhaps about shared human instincts to interact with the landscape in meaningful ways. Moreover, the various architectural styles and construction techniques used reflect the diversity of human ingenuity across different times and places.

In summary, stone circles are a global phenomenon, scattered across continents and nestled in various cultural landscapes. Their ubiquity presents a compelling narrative not just of isolated civilizations, but of a human race united by common threads of curiosity, spirituality, and an inherent desire to decode the cosmos.

SECTION 1.3: PUBLIC INTEREST AND POPULAR CULTURE

Stone circles, those ancient arrangements of large rocks, do more than just adorn landscapes and mystify archaeologists; they have also captivated the public imagination. The enigmatic nature of these structures, combined with their undeniable historical significance, has led to their feature in various aspects of popular culture—from folklore to modern media. This widespread fascination gives rise to important conversations about heritage, spirituality, and even tourism, cementing the position of stone circles as enduring icons in contemporary society.

Folklore and Traditional Narratives

The folklore that surrounds stone circles often acts as a rich tapestry of human experience and beliefs, interwoven with historical events and natural phenomena. In the British Isles, for example, legends often associate these circles with magical beings like druids or fairies. In some stories, they are the petrified remnants of people who dared to dance on a Sunday. Meanwhile, in African cultures, stone circles are sometimes thought to be the dwelling places of ancestral spirits. These stories not only add an extra layer of fascination but also serve as valuable cultural artifacts, preserving traditional worldviews and local histories for posterity.

In Modern Media

Modern media has played a significant role in popularizing the mystique surrounding stone circles. Films, books, and even video games often utilize these ancient structures as settings for magical or transformative events. The hit TV series "Outlander" and the children's classic "The Sword in the Stone" are only two examples where stone circles provide a backdrop for time travel or mystical transformations. This recurring theme highlights our collective sense that these formations are imbued with otherworldly or at least extraordinary properties.

In Music and Art

Beyond the written word and the silver screen, stone circles have inspired countless works of art and music. Some artists have used the circle motifs and the megaliths as powerful symbols of unity, eternity, or natural beauty. Musicians from various genres have also used imagery or acoustic properties of these stone circles to inform their compositions. For example, some ambient music pieces are designed to evoke the echoes or resonances that might be heard within an actual stone circle, connecting the listener with a sense of the sacred and ancient.

Spirituality and New Age Movements

The spiritual dimension of stone circles can't be ignored. For many people, these circles serve as a focus for meditation or spiritual rituals. New Age philosophies, in particular, have adopted stone circles as sites of power where the veil between the physical and spiritual worlds is thin. Pilgrimages to famous circles like Stonehenge during solstices or equinoxes have become increasingly popular, with people hoping to tap into the energies that these ancient stones are believed to channel.

Tourism and Heritage Sites

Today, many stone circles are recognized as significant heritage sites and have become popular tourist attractions. The dual role of these circles—as both archaeological wonders and symbols of cultural mythology—makes them appealing to a broad range of people. Academic researchers, history buffs, spiritual seekers, and curious tourists all find something to attract them to these ancient sites. Organizations and local governments are becoming increasingly invested in preserving these circles, not just as historic monuments but as key elements in the cultural and even economic well-being of a region.

In summary, the allure of stone circles extends far beyond their historical and geographical origins. They have been, and continue to be, fertile grounds for the human imagination, inspiring everything from local legends to blockbuster movies. Whether we are drawn to them for their history, spirituality, or the simple aesthetic pleasure they offer, one thing is clear: stone circles capture a unique and multifaceted place in our collective consciousness. As we delve deeper into their structural intricacies, archaeological significance, and speculative theories, this fascination is unlikely to wane.

CHAPTER 2: TYPES OF STONE CIRCLES

Section 2.1: Recumbent Stone Circles

In the captivating landscape of megalithic stone circles, one variation holds a particular intrigue: Recumbent Stone Circles. These feature a horizontal stone, often of massive proportions, which lies 'recumbent' or flat between two vertical 'flanker' stones. This chapter delves into the distinct features, historical significance, and regional prominence of Recumbent Stone Circles, enriching our understanding of these unique megalithic formations.

Distinctive Features

Recumbent Stone Circles are predominantly recognized by their eponymous recumbent stone, which is a large, horizontal stone, usually situated on the southern edge of the circle. It is flanked on either side by tall, vertical stones, thus creating a sort of triad that breaks the continuity of the surrounding circle. The recumbent stone itself is often carefully chosen for its texture, color, or material composition, and in some instances, it has been observed to weigh up to 20 tons or more.

Regional Prominence

These types of stone circles are particularly prevalent in northeastern Scotland, especially in areas such as Aberdeenshire. There are about 100 Recumbent Stone Circles documented in this region alone. While their distribution seems largely confined to northeastern Scotland, some have been discovered in southwestern Ireland and a few other locales. The regional specificity suggests that these stone circles were likely linked to a particular cultural or social practice unique to the inhabitants of those areas.

Archaeological Significance

From an archaeological standpoint, Recumbent Stone Circles offer a rich field for research. Excavations within and around these circles have often unearthed charcoal, cremated human bones, and pottery fragments. These findings lead researchers to propose that the sites may have been used for ritualistic purposes, perhaps connected to funerary rites. However, the evidence is not conclusive, and the actual purpose remains a topic of active academic inquiry. There are also discussions around the circles' possible astronomical functions, with some suggesting that the positioning of the recumbent stone might align with lunar or solar cycles, although this is still a subject of debate.

Connection to Folklore

The recumbent stone, being such a visually striking element, has often entered local folklore and myth. In Scotland, for instance, these stones are sometimes referred to as "Odin Stones," linked to the Norse god Odin, although no definitive Norse connection has been established. Other folklore relates these recumbent stones to giants who once roamed the lands, attributing the placement of such massive stones to these mythical beings. While the factual basis of these stories may be uncertain, they nonetheless add layers of cultural richness and imaginative scope to the enigma of Recumbent Stone Circles.

Interpretations and Theories

Various theories have been postulated to explain the presence of the recumbent stone, including but not limited to, its role in social ceremonies, agricultural festivals, or even as a territorial marker. Some theories also hint at a cosmological aspect, suggesting that the stone's horizontal position may be aligned to capture the rising or setting of celestial bodies, serving as an ancient astronomical observatory. However, none of these theories has gained universal acceptance and they often overlap or even contradict one another, making Recumbent Stone Circles a continually compelling subject for scholars, archaeologists, and enthusiasts alike.

In summary, Recumbent Stone Circles represent a unique and regionally specific type of megalithic stone circle. While their most defining feature is the horizontal recumbent stone, the questions surrounding their purpose and significance are as layered as the stones themselves. Whether looked at through the lens of archaeology, folklore, or theoretical interpretation, these intriguing structures offer a multitude of pathways for understanding not just the circle, but perhaps the circle of life and death, time, and space, that they have silently witnessed for millennia.

SECTION 2.2:
CONCENTRIC CIRCLES

Stone circles often evoke an aura of timeless enigma, and none more so than those featuring concentric circles. These stone formations are not just one simple ring but are made up of multiple rings placed inside one another, creating a ripple effect of stones emanating from a central point. The allure of concentric circles is not just in their visually arresting design but also in the complexity of their construction and their potential ritualistic or astronomical significance. Let's delve into the fascinating world of concentric stone circles, from their structural characteristics to the theories that attempt to explain their existence.

Structural Characteristics

Concentric stone circles differ from their single-ring counterparts not just in their multiple rings but often also in the types and sizes of stones used. The outermost ring typically comprises the largest stones, with the size generally decreasing toward the center. This gradation suggests a possible hierarchical or symbolic importance to the arrangement, although interpretations remain speculative. The distance between the individual rings can vary but is usually consistent within the same circle, leading some experts to believe that these distances might have a standardized or ceremonial meaning.

Geographical Distribution

Concentric stone circles are not as widespread as single-ring formations, but they still appear in diverse geographical locations. Examples include the "Circles of Senegambia" in West Africa, the "Hurlers" in Cornwall, and certain formations in the Orkney Islands of Scotland. The regional variations often reflect the local geology, with the types of stones used differing based on what was readily available. This localized adaptation provides a compelling testament to the cultural exchange of construction techniques and ritualistic practices.

Construction Challenges

The construction of concentric stone circles was no small feat. Transporting the stones, often from quarries many miles away, required an organized labor force and sophisticated tools and methods, such as levers, sledges, and possibly even rudimentary cranes. The task of aligning multiple rings accurately suggests an advanced understanding of geometry and measurement, further hinting at the high level of skill and planning involved. The concentric layout could have also required a more extensive workforce and longer timeframe to complete, as compared to single-ring formations.

Archaeological Theories

The complexity of concentric stone circles has given rise to a multitude of theories. Some suggest they served as ceremonial centers for religious rites, where the multiple rings may have been used for different aspects of a ritual. Others propose that they had astronomical functions, serving as complex calendars or celestial observatories. Still, others posit that the inner and outer circles could represent different realms—earthly and divine, for example —and that the act of moving from one circle to another could signify a spiritual transition.

Cultural and Symbolic Interpretations

The design of concentric stone circles offers fertile ground for interpretation. In various cultures, circles within circles have represented everything from the cycles of life and seasons to spiritual ascension. These symbolic associations may have been known to the builders, influencing the design and purposes of these ancient structures. Folklore often imbues these sites with mystical attributes, such as serving as portals to other realms or focusing points for spiritual energy. While these beliefs are hard to substantiate, they add another layer to our understanding of the multifaceted roles that these circles may have played in ancient societies.

In summary, concentric stone circles are an intricate variation of the more commonly found single-ring stone circles. Their complex design, labor-intensive construction, and broad geographical distribution all add dimensions of mystery and significance. While their exact purpose remains a subject of debate, the theories that have been put forward often overlap and can be complementary rather than mutually exclusive. These enthralling structures continue to captivate researchers and enthusiasts alike, and as we dig deeper—both literally and figuratively—we edge closer to unraveling the manifold secrets they hold.

SECTION 2.3: HENGES AND ASSOCIATED STRUCTURES

In this section, we will delve into the specific variations of stone circles known as henges and other related structural forms. Henges stand apart because they often feature an earthwork enclosure with a circular bank and an internal ditch. They offer intriguing insights into how our ancestors conceived of space and sacred sites.

The Definition of a Henge

A henge is an ancient structure consisting primarily of a flat area enclosed by a bank and internal ditch, with one or more entrances leading in. Unlike ordinary stone circles, where the primary focus is on the megaliths themselves, a henge centers on the relationship between the earthwork and any stones or wooden posts that may be present. Typically, henges were constructed during the Neolithic period, roughly from 5000 BC to 2000 BC. The earthworks serve to separate the internal space from the outside world, making it a secluded, special area.

Henges versus Ordinary Stone Circles

It's essential to make a distinction between henges and simple stone circles. While all henges are enclosures, not all enclosures are henges. For instance, a simple stone circle might consist only of megaliths arranged in a ring without the defining earthworks characteristic of a henge. Moreover, while henges may contain stone circles or wooden posts, their presence is not necessary for a structure to be considered a henge. Some henges, like the famous Stonehenge, include complex interior arrangements of stones, yet the term "henge" technically refers only to the outer earthworks, emphasizing the importance of the surrounding landscape in defining these structures.

Variations in Henge Structures

There are various types of henge structures that one might encounter in archaeological landscapes. While the traditional henge features a single bank and ditch, some variations exist. For instance, "hengiforms" mimic the basic layout of a henge but may lack the full features, such as complete circularity or an internal ditch. Other variants like "super henges," exemplified by structures like Durrington Walls near Stonehenge, encompass a much larger area and could have supported a sizable community within their boundaries. These variations suggest that the concept of a henge was flexible and adapted to suit local needs and landscapes.

Regional Differences

Henges are most commonly found in the British Isles, though they do exist in other parts of Europe. In fact, regional variations often provide clues to the site's original purpose. For example, the timber circles within henges in England might suggest ritualistic activities involving large gatherings, whereas in Scotland, smaller stone circles within henges could imply a more intimate, perhaps familial, usage. Regional differences also extend to the materials used for construction, the alignment with celestial bodies, and even the number and types of entrances, all of which contribute to our understanding of these enigmatic structures.

Henges and Associated Ritualistic Elements

Beyond their structural differences, henges often feature a variety of associated elements that hint at their usage. These might include burial mounds, post holes, pits, or even artefacts like pottery shards and animal bones. Such findings suggest that henges were not just architectural feats but served functional, often ritualistic, purposes. For example, the presence of animal bones and charcoal could indicate sacrifices or communal feasts. Additionally, the orientation of the entrances often aligns with celestial events, supporting the idea that astronomical observations were integrated into the ritualistic activities conducted at these sites.

In summary, henges add another layer to our understanding of stone circles by introducing the element of earthworks and the relationships between these and any interior structures. Their variations and regional differences point towards a rich tapestry of ancient cultural practices and beliefs. While stone circles captivate us through their simplicity and elegance, henges intrigue us by their complexity and their ability to offer a multifaceted glimpse into the past.

CHAPTER 3: ARCHAEOLOGICAL THEORIES AND DEBATES

Section 3.1: Early Theories

Understanding the mysteries shrouded around stone circles involves diving into a wide array of theories and interpretations. Over the decades, scholars have postulated a variety of ideas regarding the purpose and functionality of these ancient structures. In this section, we'll focus on early theories stemming from the 20th-century archaeological landscape. These theories laid the foundation for the multifaceted discussion that surrounds stone circles today.

Antiquarian Perspectives

In the early 20th century, much of the study around stone circles was confined to the observations made by antiquarians. These were people who engaged in the study of antiquities or ancient times but were not always formally trained in archaeological methods. Antiquarian theories were often anecdotal and speculative, focusing on the aesthetic and superficial qualities of the stone circles. For example, it was not uncommon for antiquarians to connect these structures with local myths and folklore, an approach that was limited in its scientific rigour but captivated public imagination.

Archaeoastronomy

One of the early scientific theories about stone circles was related to archaeoastronomy. Early 20th-century scholars like Sir Norman Lockyer posited that these structures could have been used as primitive calendars or celestial observatories. The idea was based on the alignment of certain stones with the rising and setting of celestial bodies like the sun, moon, and even some stars. These theories set the stage for a more methodological approach to the study of megalithic structures, even though the limitations of technology at the time restricted comprehensive verification.

Cultural and Ritualistic Interpretations

The early part of the 20th century also witnessed theories that attributed a socio-cultural and ritualistic purpose to these stone circles. Researchers like Margaret Murray speculated that these circles could be linked to forms of ancestor worship or were places for religious and social gatherings. These theories were often derived from the accounts of classical historians and ethnographic comparisons with indigenous cultures. The limitations here were the lack of concrete evidence, such as inscriptions or ritual artifacts, to decisively support such theories.

Practical Utilities

Another strand of theories focused on the practical utilities of these stone circles. Some scholars, like O.G.S. Crawford, posited that the stones could have been territorial markers or had functions related to agriculture, like being sophisticated forms of cattle pens. Such utilitarian views, though not as glamorous as ritualistic or astronomical interpretations, provided an essential balance in the early debates surrounding the purpose of these ancient structures.

Debunking of Older Views

As archaeology matured as a discipline, there was an increasing move towards empiricism and the scientific method. By the middle of the 20th century, many earlier theories were subjected to scrutiny and were either refined or debunked. The advent of radiocarbon dating, for instance, allowed for more accurate dating of organic materials found at these sites, often discrediting earlier speculative timelines. Newer methodologies in landscape archaeology also paved the way for a more nuanced understanding of the stone circles and their context.

In summary, the early theories of the 20th century served as both a catalyst and a foundation for subsequent research into stone circles. Despite the limitations inherent in these initial hypotheses, they sparked the curiosity and debate that have led to the more nuanced, multidisciplinary approaches we see today. From speculative antiquarian perspectives to the beginnings of a more empirical, scientific methodology, these early views have shaped the rich tapestry of understanding that continues to evolve in the study of these enigmatic structures.

SECTION 3.2:
RITUALISTIC USE

When contemplating the ancient stone circles that embellish landscapes across various parts of the world, one of the most frequently pondered questions concerns their purpose. While numerous theories exist, ranging from practical to esoteric, the possibility that these megalithic structures were primarily used for religious or ritualistic activities remains one of the most compelling hypotheses. This section will explore the evidence and scholarly discussions that surround the theory of stone circles being spaces of ritualistic importance.

One key argument in favor of a ritualistic function is the presence of burial sites within or near many stone circles. For instance, at Avebury in Wiltshire, England, human remains have been discovered, which have been dated to the same era as the stones. Similar burial contexts are found in other megalithic sites, such as the Ring of Brodgar in Scotland. While burial alone does not necessarily confirm a religious function, it is a potent indication that these were spaces of special significance, often encompassing the spheres of life, death, and possibly an afterlife.

Another pointer towards the ritualistic usage of stone circles comes from the artifacts found at these sites. Items like pottery, animal bones, and fragments of metal often exhibit signs of ceremonial deposition. That is, they seem to have been placed deliberately, rather than simply discarded. This indicates a controlled and thoughtful interaction with the space, which is often associated with ritualistic activities. Moreover, the type of artifacts, especially those related to communal feasting or sacrifice, further supports the idea that these sites were places of communal gathering for ceremonial purposes.

Archaeologists have also explored the concept of "liminality" in the context of stone circles. In anthropological terms, liminality refers to the a specific quality of ambiguity or disorientation that often occurs in the middle stage of a ritual. Stone circles, in their geometrically defined, yet open enclosures, can serve as liminal spaces where participants transition from one state to another, be it spiritual, social, or psychological. The very architecture of these circles, therefore, may have been designed to facilitate such transformative experiences.

However, it is essential to note that not all scholars are in agreement about the ritualistic interpretation. Critics point out that concrete evidence is scanty and largely circumstantial. The presence of human remains or artifacts could have alternate explanations such as simple proximity to settlements or even later usage of the site for various purposes. Additionally, there is the challenge of "reading" ancient ritualistic practices through the limited lens of contemporary understanding, a process fraught with the risk of projecting modern beliefs onto prehistoric contexts.

Ethnographic comparisons with indigenous cultures who utilize stone circles or similar structures for ritualistic purposes provide some additional grounding for this theory. For example, Native American medicine wheels and African stone circle traditions often serve ritualistic functions, suggesting that the concept of using stone configurations for spiritual or social ceremonies is not confined to a single culture or era.

Despite the criticisms and alternative theories, the idea that stone circles had a ritualistic function is well-entrenched in both scholarly discussions and public imagination. This may be partly because the notion resonates with the human inclination to ascribe meaning to mysterious structures, especially when they require significant communal effort to create, as is the case with these megaliths.

In summary, while definitive proof remains elusive, the weight of circumstantial evidence, combined with comparative ethnographic studies, leans favorably towards the theory that stone circles were used for ritualistic purposes. Whether serving as sacred burial grounds, spaces for communal gathering, or transformative liminal stages, these enigmatic structures continue to captivate us as we seek to understand the spiritual and social dynamics of ancient civilizations.

SECTION 3.3: ASTRONOMICAL THEORIES

The study of stone circles has branched into many specialized areas, including history, anthropology, and geology. However, one of the most captivating perspectives on these ancient structures comes from the field of astronomy. In this section, we will explore the fascinating theories that posit stone circles as early astronomical tools.

Megalithic Observatories

The notion that stone circles were used for astronomical purposes was popularized in academic discussions in the 20th century. The famous British astronomer Sir Fred Hoyle was among those who presented the idea that ancient societies used these structures as observational platforms. By aligning stones in particular configurations, they could note the movements of celestial bodies, including the Sun, Moon, and even some stars. The idea suggests that these circles were ancient calendars, enabling ancient communities to predict seasons, equinoxes, and solstices. This astronomical alignment theory is supported by the orientation of many stone circles towards significant celestial events, such as the midsummer sunrise at Stonehenge.

Lunar Cycles and Stone Circles

While the solar calendar is the more widely accepted concept today, ancient societies also paid close attention to the Moon. The lunar cycle, especially the phases of the Moon, holds significant importance in some theories related to stone circles. Some stone circles, like Callanish in Scotland, appear to have been aligned with lunar standstill events, which occur every 18.6 years. These alignments have led scholars to speculate that the circles could have functioned as lunar calendars, tracking the intricate cycles of the Moon and perhaps providing a basis for ritualistic activities synchronized with these cycles.

Ecliptic and Stellar Alignments

Although the Sun and Moon dominate much of the astronomical interpretations of stone circles, some theories go a step further and suggest that certain circles are aligned with specific stars or star clusters. For example, some alignments with the Pleiades and Sirius have been proposed. While these theories are debated and often met with skepticism, there is merit in examining the possibility that ancient civilizations had an intricate understanding of the night sky.

Archaeoastronomy: The Interdisciplinary Approach

Archaeoastronomy is the interdisciplinary field that combines archaeological and astronomical methods to study ancient cultures. Researchers in this field use sophisticated techniques like computer modeling to understand how stone circles would have aligned with celestial bodies at the time they were built. These models often take into account the Earth's axial precession, a phenomenon where the orientation of Earth's axis changes over time. By doing so, they aim to offer a more nuanced interpretation of these structures, considering not only their physical layout but also their potential functionality as ancient observatories.

The Debate and Skepticism

While the astronomical theories related to stone circles have a large following, they also face skepticism. Critics argue that the alignments may be coincidental and that attributing sophisticated astronomical knowledge to ancient societies without concrete evidence is speculative. Moreover, the absence of written records from the time these structures were built complicates the matter. However, the debate itself is valuable as it pushes for more comprehensive research, bringing in a wide range of methodologies, from satellite imaging to ancient texts, to understand these enigmatic formations better.

In summary, the astronomical theories surrounding stone circles offer a compelling lens through which to view these mysterious structures. Whether serving as calendars or observatories, the notion that they were used to connect with celestial phenomena adds another layer to our understanding of ancient cultures and their interaction with the cosmos. While questions and debates persist, the intersection of archaeology and astronomy provides a fruitful ground for ongoing research, promising deeper insights in the years to come.

CHAPTER 4: ARCHITECTURAL ASPECTS

Section 4.1: Material and Construction

Stone circles, fascinating relics of the past, have long captured our imagination not just for their mystical allure but also for their architectural ingenuity. Their construction required meticulous planning, an understanding of materials, and considerable manual labor. This section delves into the types of stones used in these structures and the methods employed to erect them.

Types of Stones Used

The choice of stone varied widely depending on the geographic location of the stone circle. In the British Isles, for instance, sarsen stones were a popular choice for many structures, including the iconic Stonehenge. These are sandstone blocks that were probably sourced locally. In other regions, such as the Senegambian Stone Circles in West Africa, laterite stones were more commonly used. The key factors in stone selection typically included availability, durability, and ease of shaping.

Notably, some stone circles feature a variety of stones. The reason behind this is still a matter of debate among archaeologists. Some speculate that the different stones could have held varying symbolic meanings. Others suggest that the choice could have been more practical, driven by the properties of each type of stone —some might be more suitable for vertical elements, while others would work better as capstones.

Quarrying and Shaping

Extracting large stones from quarries was a labor-intensive task that required significant manpower and ingenuity. Several methods might have been employed, such as the use of wooden wedges that were inserted into cracks and soaked with water. As the wood expanded, it would crack the stone, allowing it to be more easily extracted. After quarrying, the stones were shaped using harder stone tools, and in some instances, metal chisels, though these were less common due to the scarcity of metal during the periods these structures were generally erected.

Transportation Methods

Transporting the quarried stones to the construction site is one of the most baffling aspects of stone circle construction. Various theories suggest the use of sledges, rollers, or even waterways to move these massive rocks. The transportation process often required community collaboration. Rituals and ceremonies were possibly associated with this task, adding a spiritual dimension to what would have been a significant engineering challenge.

In the case of Stonehenge, some stones are believed to have been transported from as far away as Wales, a feat that would have required a highly organized effort. How exactly this was achieved remains a topic of ongoing research and discussion.

Construction Techniques

Once at the construction site, the stones had to be erected—a daunting task given their size and weight. Likely, a combination of ramps, levers, and counterweights was used. Shallow holes, known as "stone holes," were dug to provide a stable base for the upright stones. The method for positioning the lintels or capstones on top of upright stones varied but could have involved the construction of temporary wooden scaffolding or earthen ramps.

It is important to note that the construction of stone circles would likely have had ceremonial aspects as well. The selection of the site, the specific orientation of the stones, and the time of year during which construction activities took place might all have been deeply symbolic, possibly aligned with celestial events or seasonal changes.

In summary, the construction of stone circles was an intricate process that required a deep understanding of materials and a high degree of coordination and skill. From the initial selection and extraction of stones to their eventual arrangement in the circle, each step was fraught with challenges that the builders somehow overcame. Whether driven by practical needs, spiritual beliefs, or a combination of both, these ancient marvels stand as testaments to the capabilities of their creators, echoing across the centuries with whispers of forgotten knowledge and skill.

SECTION 4.2: SPATIAL ORIENTATION

In the realm of stone circles, it's not just the types of stones used or the physical arrangement that catches the attention of researchers, historians, and spiritual enthusiasts. Another fascinating aspect lies in their spatial orientation. These enigmatic formations often seem to be meticulously aligned with certain natural features and celestial bodies, compelling us to look beyond mere coincidence.

Alignments with Celestial Bodies

One of the most captivating aspects of stone circles is their alignment with celestial bodies. For instance, Stonehenge, perhaps the most famous of all stone circles, is aligned so that the heel stone marks the spot on the horizon where the sun rises during the summer solstice. Similarly, other circles have been found to align with the winter solstice, equinoxes, and even specific star constellations.

Various theories suggest that these alignments had ritualistic or calendrical purposes. Some researchers propose that these circles served as ancient observatories or calendars. By marking crucial solar or lunar events, communities could time their agricultural activities, religious rituals, and social gatherings. The understanding of such alignments has evolved over time, gaining scholarly acceptance, especially due to the increased interest in archaeoastronomy—a field that explores how past societies understood celestial phenomena and how they incorporated this understanding into their cultures.

Alignment with Terrestrial Features

The spatial orientation of stone circles also often corresponds with specific features in the landscape. For example, some stone circles align with nearby mountains, rivers, or other notable geographical markers. The Ring of Brodgar in Scotland is set within a natural circle of water, aligning its construction with the nearby lochs. In some cases, the circles are aligned with more distant landmarks, sometimes visible only from a high vantage point.

The reasons behind these alignments remain a subject of scholarly debate. Some suggest that they serve to connect human-made structures with the natural world, creating a harmonious balance between the built and natural environments. Others propose more practical purposes like navigation or territorial marking. Whatever the reasons, these alignments add another layer of complexity to the already enigmatic nature of stone circles.

Magnetic Alignments

Another dimension of spatial orientation is magnetic alignment. Some stone circles are oriented along the Earth's magnetic field lines. This phenomenon is less understood and requires multidisciplinary study, including geophysics and archaeology. Some theories postulate that ancient societies had knowledge of the Earth's magnetic field and used it for purposes such as navigation or even mystical rituals.

Mathematical and Geometrical Arrangements

While it may seem like an anachronism, there is evidence to suggest that ancient builders used complex mathematical and geometrical knowledge in the construction of some stone circles. For example, certain formations show precise equidistant spacing between stones, and some even exhibit spirals and other complex geometric shapes.

The reasons for these precise arrangements are not entirely clear. Some researchers suggest that these might represent a form of ancient "coding," a way to pass on astronomical, calendrical, or even spiritual knowledge. The use of geometry and mathematics in the construction of these circles could indicate a far more advanced understanding of these subjects than previously thought.

Summary

The spatial orientation of stone circles is a captivating subject, providing rich material for multidisciplinary study. From alignments with celestial bodies to corresponding with natural features of the landscape, the placement and orientation of these ancient structures appear to be anything but arbitrary. Whether for astronomical, ritualistic, or still-unknown purposes, these alignments invite further study and appreciation. They enrich our understanding of the stone circles as not just isolated ancient artifacts but as carefully designed installations that interact in complex ways with their surroundings and perhaps even the cosmos.

SECTION 4.3: ACOUSTIC PROPERTIES

Stone circles have fascinated us for centuries, not just for their enigmatic purpose and precise construction but also for their lesser-known attributes like acoustic properties. Some stone circles, it turns out, have very interesting sound characteristics that could possibly shed light on their ritualistic or functional use.

The "Sonic" Stones of Stonehenge

One of the most famous examples illustrating the acoustic attributes of megalithic structures is Stonehenge. Researchers have found that the bluestones at this iconic site possess particular resonant qualities. These bluestones, imported from quarries in Wales, ring when struck, much like a bell. Theories suggest that this property was well known to the ancient builders and was one of the reasons for choosing these stones over others. One could imagine a scenario where striking these stones formed part of ritualistic activities, thereby adding an auditory dimension to the already complex layers of Stonehenge's significance.

Sound Reverberation in Other Circles

Stonehenge is not the only stone circle with intriguing acoustic properties. Other circles like the Ring of Brodgar in Scotland and certain Irish stone circles also show evidence of sound-related characteristics. These may involve sound reverberation, echo effects, and even what is termed as "whispering galleries," where a whisper on one side can be clearly heard at a great distance on the opposite side. These phenomena are often closely linked to the stones' composition, arrangement, and even the surrounding landscape.

Scientific Examinations of Acoustics

Understanding the acoustic attributes of stone circles has become an exciting interdisciplinary field, bringing together archaeologists, sound engineers, and even musicians. Some researchers employ advanced technology such as acoustic modeling software to simulate how sound would have behaved within these ancient structures. These simulations allow for the exploration of questions regarding the intended acoustic experience, how sound could be manipulated for ceremonies, or whether these sites were early examples of engineered "concert halls."

Sound and Ritualistic Implications

Many theories suggest that the acoustic properties of stone circles might have been intentionally engineered for ritualistic or ceremonial purposes. For instance, the nature of sound reverberation could have been significant in religious ceremonies to create an ethereal or mystical experience. Musical instruments, like drums or flutes, might have been played in conjunction with the resonant stones to achieve a desired acoustic effect. This combination of natural and man-made sounds could offer a multisensory ritual experience, augmenting the spiritual significance of these sites.

Comparing Stone Circles and Modern Architecture

Interestingly, modern architecture also employs similar principles of acoustics, although for different purposes such as optimizing concert halls or quieting busy urban environments. In this context, the acoustic properties of stone circles underscore how our ancient predecessors were keen observers and manipulators of their environment, albeit with limited technological means. They demonstrate a deep understanding of how sound interacts with materials and space, an understanding that has been corroborated and built upon by modern science.

In summary, the acoustic properties of stone circles offer an intriguing avenue for research and interpretation. While not universally present in all stone circles, where these properties do exist, they open up a world of questions about the builders' intentions, the circle's uses, and even the experiences of those who interacted with these spaces. From Stonehenge's bluestones that ring like bells to the whispering galleries of other circles, the sonic characteristics add yet another layer to the complex tapestry of human ingenuity and the enduring allure of these ancient structures.

CHAPTER 5: LEY LINES AND ENERGY VORTICES

Section 5.1: Introduction to Ley Lines

Ley lines are a captivating subject that intersects with the world of stone circles in a fascinating way. The term "ley lines" originates from the British landscape, specifically coined by amateur archaeologist Alfred Watkins in the early 20th century. Watkins posited that these invisible lines crisscross the Earth, linking different geographical features, historical landmarks, and, notably for our discussion, stone circles. The notion of ley lines offers an esoteric dimension to our understanding of these ancient structures, although it should be noted that scientific evidence supporting the existence of ley lines remains scant.

The Origin and Evolution of the Ley Line Concept

Alfred Watkins, a businessman with a keen interest in history and archaeology, is credited with introducing the concept of ley lines to modern thought. In 1921, while surveying the Herefordshire landscape in England, he noticed that various landmarks, such as churches, mounds, and stone circles, seemed to align in straight lines. Watkins surmised that these alignments were neither coincidental nor random but were part of an ancient system of navigation used by prehistoric peoples. He proposed that these lines once served as trading routes, or "leys," and hence the name "ley lines."

However, the interpretation of ley lines has evolved over time. Some proponents have imbued them with mystical or spiritual significance. These advocates suggest that ley lines are currents of energy flowing through the Earth, connecting not just physical locations but also linking the cosmic and spiritual realms. This perception has given rise to a variety of beliefs and practices that consider ley lines as conduits of life force, akin to the "chi" in Chinese philosophy or "prana" in Indian traditions.

Ley Lines and Stone Circles: A Confluence of Mysteries

The intersection of ley lines with stone circles is a subject of ongoing debate and fascination. Certain alignments do seem to connect multiple ancient sites, including stone circles. For instance, the "Michael Line" in England, a well-known ley, aligns with several Neolithic sites and stone circles. Likewise, many stone circles in the British Isles, such as Avebury and Stonehenge, are often cited as nodes on complex networks of ley lines.

These alignments have led to numerous theories. Some speculate that the ancients erected these stone circles to mark or harness the energy flowing through these lines. Others wonder if the stone circles might have served as ritualistic sites where these energies were invoked or manipulated. However, it's essential to note that no scientific evidence has conclusively verified these ideas.

Critiques and Counterarguments

Skeptics of ley lines often point to the lack of specific empirical data and methodological rigor in their study. They argue that any set of random points can be connected to form a straight line, and thus the perceived alignments might merely be coincidental. This criticism also extends to the supposed connection between stone circles and ley lines. Critics argue that since stone circles themselves are spread out over vast regions, it is statistically likely that some would intersect with so-called ley lines by mere chance.

That said, the topic of ley lines and their connection to stone circles continues to captivate researchers, history enthusiasts, and those with a penchant for the mysterious. Regardless of one's stance on their existence or significance, ley lines add an intriguing layer to the already complex and enigmatic nature of stone circles.

Summary

In this section, we have delved into the captivating subject of ley lines and their intersection with stone circles. Originating as an observational theory by Alfred Watkins in the early 20th century, ley lines have become enmeshed in both mystical beliefs and contentious debates. While some intriguing alignments between stone circles and purported ley lines exist, no definitive scientific evidence supports the more esoteric claims about their connection. Nevertheless, the allure of ley lines persists, enriching the tapestry of mysteries that surround stone circles.

SECTION 5.2:
ENERGY VORTICES

In our journey through the fascinating world of stone circles, ley lines have made their mark as intriguing geometrical alignments that some say connect ancient landmarks. However, the mysteries don't stop there. Along these ley lines and even within the stone circles themselves, another captivating concept surfaces—energy vortices. This section will explore what energy vortices are, the theories and beliefs surrounding their existence, and whether any scientific evidence supports these claims.

What Are Energy Vortices?

An energy vortex, in the context of mystical beliefs and alternative theories, is said to be a concentrated area where energy flows in a spiral, clockwise or counter-clockwise motion. The concept is deeply embedded in various traditions and spiritual practices, from Eastern philosophies like Hinduism and Buddhism, which speak of chakras and energy centers, to New Age spirituality that advocates the existence of Earth's energy hotspots. While these beliefs are deeply ingrained in cultural and spiritual contexts, it's essential to point out that mainstream scientific paradigms do not currently recognize energy vortices as quantifiable or measurable phenomena.

Energy Vortices and Stone Circles

The notion that stone circles could serve as conduits for these energy vortices is captivating to many. Proponents of this idea argue that the placement of these stones is no coincidence, but rather a deliberate act designed to harness or mark these unique energy spots. Several dowsers and independent researchers have claimed to identify unusual energy readings or sensations when near or within stone circles. These individuals often use divining rods, pendulums, and even specialized electrical equipment to demonstrate these findings. It is, however, important to consider that these methodologies are not universally accepted within the scientific community.

Theories and Explanations

Among those who endorse the concept of energy vortices, explanations for their presence at stone circle sites vary. Some suggest that these energy centers have a healing effect, attracting individuals in search of physical or spiritual well-being. Others propose that the energy flow could have practical purposes, such as enhancing the fertility of the land or aiding in navigation. More esoteric theories even suggest that these vortices could serve as portals or gateways to other dimensions. Again, while these ideas are rich in imagination and offer a sense of wonder, they do not have empirical validation through peer-reviewed scientific studies.

Geomagnetic Anomalies: A Scientific Perspective

Though the concept of energy vortices doesn't find a footing in mainstream scientific thought, it's worth noting that geomagnetic anomalies do exist. These are areas where the Earth's magnetic field shows marked variations. While some stone circles coincide with such anomalies, researchers are cautious to not leap to mystical interpretations. Instead, geomagnetic studies often focus on geological explanations such as variations in the Earth's crust or the presence of mineral deposits. To date, there is no conclusive evidence linking these magnetic variations to the mystical energy vortices as described by alternative theories.

Skepticism and Balanced Views

While the notion of energy vortices may stir curiosity and even fervor among some, it's important to remember that these ideas rest largely on personal beliefs and anecdotal evidence. Some critics argue that the sensations or 'energies' people feel at these sites are psychological effects, perhaps triggered by the site's aesthetic or historical significance. Moreover, the scientific community, operating on empirical evidence, does not endorse these concepts, considering them speculative until proven otherwise.

In summary, energy vortices, as they are commonly understood in mystical and New Age contexts, offer an intriguing but controversial layer to the discussion of stone circles. While they capture the imagination and are the subject of various anecdotal claims, they lack empirical support from the scientific establishment. Regardless of one's perspective, these alleged phenomena contribute to the sense of mystery and awe that many feel when visiting or studying stone circles, making them an enduring part of the conversation.

SECTION 5.3:
SKEPTICISM AND
SCIENTIFIC SCRUTINY

Ley lines and energy vortices are intriguing concepts that have stirred imaginations and incited debates in both popular and academic circles. As with any subject that carries an air of the mysterious or esoteric, it's important to look at these phenomena through a lens of scientific scrutiny. In this section, we'll examine some of the criticisms and evaluations from the scientific community concerning the claims related to ley lines and energy vortices in connection with stone circles.

Defining the Parameters of Inquiry

To examine these phenomena critically, it's crucial to define what exactly is being claimed. Ley lines are often described as invisible pathways of energy that crisscross the Earth, linking diverse sacred sites and natural formations. Energy vortices are said to be powerful energy centers where ley lines intersect. Critics point out that these definitions can be rather vague, making them difficult to test or disprove. For scientific inquiry to proceed, definitions must be specific and claims must be falsifiable.

Lack of Empirical Evidence

The scientific method is grounded in empirical evidence— observable, measurable data collected through experiment or observation. Despite anecdotal reports, there's a notable lack of robust empirical evidence to support the existence of ley lines and energy vortices. While various devices, like dowsing rods, have been employed to detect these energies, their efficacy is often questioned by the scientific community.

Skepticism from Geology and Physics

Geologists and physicists are often skeptical of the concept of ley lines and energy vortices for multiple reasons. Firstly, there's the lack of a clear mechanism that would allow these supposed energies to interact with the physical world in a measurable way. Many of the forces described in relation to ley lines do not conform to known principles of physics. Additionally, geological studies have not found any unusual underground features, like significant mineral deposits or magnetic anomalies, at many of the stone circles purportedly located on ley lines.

Evaluations in Social Sciences and Psychology

On the other hand, the field of psychology offers another avenue for scrutiny. Some psychologists suggest that the sensation of increased energy or spirituality at these sites might be a form of the placebo effect or can be attributed to the power of suggestion. The history, folklore, and pre-existing beliefs surrounding these places can influence individual experiences, making them feel more potent or mystical than they might otherwise seem.

The Importance of Multidisciplinary Approaches

While hard sciences like geology and physics might not offer much support for ley lines and energy vortices, disciplines like anthropology and sociology offer valuable perspectives. Cultural beliefs surrounding these phenomena can be as influential in shaping human behavior and interaction with these sites as any "real" energy might be. Therefore, a multidisciplinary approach that incorporates both scientific skepticism and an understanding of cultural and psychological factors can provide a more rounded understanding.

Interdisciplinary Dialogues

Many contemporary researchers advocate for a dialogue between disciplines to better understand the complexities surrounding ley lines and energy vortices. Interdisciplinary studies that incorporate geography, folklore, psychology, and even digital humanities might offer fresh perspectives. While skepticism remains a healthy and necessary part of any scientific inquiry, it's also important to be open to new methodologies and insights.

In summary, while ley lines and energy vortices captivate the imagination, they currently lack robust empirical backing from a scientific standpoint. Criticisms often center around vague definitions, a dearth of measurable evidence, and incongruities with established scientific principles. However, other disciplines like anthropology and psychology contribute additional layers of understanding, emphasizing the multifaceted nature of these phenomena. Scientific scrutiny is essential but should be accompanied by an openness to interdisciplinary inquiry to fully explore the joy, richness and complexity of the subject.

CHAPTER 6:
CULTURAL IMPACT

Section 6.1: Stone Circles in Religion and Spirituality

Stone circles have long fascinated people, not just as historical or archaeological marvels but also as spiritual and religious symbols. The air of mystery that surrounds these ancient structures has made them focal points in various modern spiritual practices and religious narratives. This section will delve into how contemporary religions and spiritual paths incorporate these stone circles, both as places of worship and as symbols laden with deeper meanings.

Neopaganism and Wicca

One of the most notable spiritual communities that actively engage with stone circles is the Neopagan and Wiccan traditions. In these paths, stone circles are often seen as sacred spaces where the Earth's energy is concentrated. Rituals like sabbats and esbats are sometimes conducted within or around these ancient structures. Participants use the space to connect with natural elements and energies, invoking gods, goddesses, and elemental spirits pertinent to their tradition. Although not all Neopagans and Wiccans use actual ancient stone circles, some build their own to serve similar spiritual functions.

Druidry

Druids, both historical and those of modern Druidry, have often been linked to stone circles, although the historical evidence for this association is debated among scholars. In contemporary Druidic practices, stone circles serve as outdoor temples where rituals, meditations, and ceremonies occur. The circles are seen as points where the divine and earthly realms intersect, making them potent locations for spiritual work.

Eastern Philosophy

While stone circles are predominantly a feature of Western landscapes, their symbolic significance has captivated individuals from various Eastern philosophies. Some interpret stone circles in the context of chakras, the energy centers in Eastern spiritual traditions. Although this interpretation is a form of cultural syncretism rather than rooted in ancient practices, it reflects the universal appeal of these structures.

New Age Spirituality

In New Age spirituality, stone circles often take on varied and eclectic meanings. They're sometimes described as portals or vortexes of energy, aligning with ley lines and meridians in the Earth. Some practitioners use the circles for meditation, healing, and even for attempting contact with higher dimensions or extraterrestrial beings. The ideas may be modern, and often subject to skepticism, but they illustrate the stone circles' enduring ability to inspire awe and wonder.

Monotheistic Religions

Though not as common, some followers of monotheistic religions also engage with stone circles. For instance, some Christians view them as places touched by the divine hand, interpreting them through a Biblical lens. Similarly, a few Islamic scholars consider the circles as ancient places of worship, perhaps linked to early Abrahamic traditions. However, mainstream religious institutions within monotheism usually do not endorse these views, and these interpretations remain the purview of a small minority.

Indigenous and Folk Beliefs

In regions where stone circles are native, indigenous and folk traditions may have their own interpretations and uses for these structures. In Africa, for example, stone circles are sometimes integrated into traditional religious practices and community rites. Similarly, in parts of Europe, local legends and folklore about witches, fairies, and giants often incorporate stone circles, though these are more cultural remnants than active religious engagements.

In sum, the cultural and spiritual footprint of stone circles is both deep and wide. These structures are not merely relics of a bygone era but continue to serve as vibrant venues for spiritual exploration and religious meaning. Whether it's the solemn Druid conducting a ceremony under the moonlight or a New Age enthusiast dowsing for earth energies, stone circles continue to be a meeting ground between the human spirit and the mysteries of the cosmos.

SECTION 6.2: TOURISM AND PRESERVATION

The allure of stone circles extends far beyond the realm of historians and archaeologists. Today, these mysterious structures attract a wide range of visitors, from tourists to spiritual seekers. While tourism offers opportunities for local economies and helps promote cultural heritage, it also presents challenges concerning the preservation and sustainability of these ancient sites. In this section, we'll delve into the tourism aspect of stone circles and its impact on their conservation.

The Economic Impact of Tourism

Tourism related to ancient monuments like stone circles is a lucrative sector for many regions. Stonehenge, which is probably one of the most iconic stone circles, draws millions of visitors each year, contributing substantially to the local economy. According to estimates, heritage tourism can bring in significant revenue, not just from ticket sales but also from associated expenditures like lodging, food, and souvenirs. The economic boost often provides much-needed funds for small communities that may lack other sources of revenue.

Educational and Interpretive Programs

Tourist sites with significant historical or cultural value

frequently offer educational programs aimed at enhancing visitor experience. Many stone circle locations offer guided tours, interactive exhibits, and workshops. For example, visitor centers often feature interpretative panels that explain the archaeological theories, cultural history, and even the myths surrounding the stone circles. Some sites also collaborate with local schools and universities to facilitate educational field trips, thereby nurturing an appreciation for cultural heritage from a young age.

Ethical Tourism

The influx of visitors can also have its drawbacks, particularly concerning the site's preservation. Foot traffic can lead to soil erosion and degradation of the stone structures over time. Some tourist activities, such as the urge to touch or climb the ancient stones, can exacerbate wear and tear. Therefore, ethical tourism, which educates visitors on how to interact responsibly with the site, is crucial. For example, clearly marked pathways, guided tours, and informative signage can aid in minimizing harm while maximizing educational value.

Preservation Efforts and Legislation

Preserving these ancient structures for future generations is an ongoing effort that often requires collaboration between various stakeholders, including governmental bodies, non-profit organizations, and local communities. Many countries have laws aimed at protecting cultural heritage sites, requiring rigorous approval processes for any construction or development near these areas. Technology like LiDAR and ground-penetrating radar also aids in monitoring the structural integrity of the sites. Funds from tourism often contribute to conservation activities, which can include anything from basic maintenance to complex structural assessments and renovations.

Balancing Tourism and Sustainability

The long-term sustainability of stone circles as tourist destinations requires a delicate balancing act between economic gain and preservation. Visitor management strategies, including ticketing systems that limit daily visitor numbers and seasonal closures for maintenance, have been effective in some locations. Investing in durable infrastructures like well-planned paths and viewing platforms can also mitigate environmental impact. Simultaneously, ongoing research helps to update best practices in preserving the sites, ensuring that they continue to generate awe and curiosity for many generations to come.

In summary, the tourism aspect of stone circles serves as both an opportunity and a challenge. While these enigmatic structures captivate the imagination and bring economic benefits, they also necessitate careful planning and management to ensure their longevity. The principles of ethical tourism and collaborative preservation efforts are crucial in maintaining the integrity of these sites, allowing them to continue playing their multifaceted roles in our cultural, historical, and spiritual landscapes.

SECTION 6.3: STONE CIRCLES IN ART AND LITERATURE

Stone circles, aside from their historical and archaeological significance, have had a profound influence on various forms of art and literature. These enigmatic structures have captured the human imagination in ways that transcend their stone composition and geographical settings, offering themselves as portals into realms of creativity, spirituality, and cultural commentary. In this section, we delve into the fascinating presence of stone circles within artistic mediums such as painting, sculpture, literature, and film.

The Romantic Movement and Visual Arts

The Romantic era, roughly spanning the late 18th to mid-19th century, was a period in which artists and intellectuals shifted their focus from the rational to the emotional and mysterious. The mysterious aura surrounding stone circles made them ripe subjects for Romantic painters. Artists like John Constable and Caspar David Friedrich incorporated these ancient structures into their landscapes, often imbuing them with a sense of the sublime. In such works, stone circles are not merely background details but play a pivotal role in setting the tone and evoking emotions. Their inclusion served to highlight themes of nature's grandeur, human insignificance, and often, the ineffable mystery of existence.

Literature and Poetry

The literary world also has not remained untouched by the allure of stone circles. The structures find mention in works ranging from epic poems to modern fantasy novels. William Wordsworth, a key literary figure in the Romantic movement, wrote extensively about Neolithic and Bronze Age monuments, including stone circles, in his poetry. Wordsworth's stone circles are often sites of reflection, spirituality, and communion with the past.

More recently, popular culture has harnessed the mystique of stone circles through genres like fantasy and science fiction. For example, Diana Gabaldon's "Outlander" series uses a stone circle as a portal through which the protagonist time travels. The choice is intentional, drawing on the real-world intrigue and myths surrounding these ancient formations to add a layer of plausibility and fascination to the narrative.

Stone Circles in Modern Art and Sculpture

The influence of stone circles extends to modern art and sculpture as well. Many contemporary artists have been inspired by the minimalist form and geometric patterns of these ancient structures. Environmental artists like Richard Long and Andy Goldsworthy have created modern stone circles in natural settings, blending the line between ancient inspiration and modern expression. These artworks often provoke discourse on themes such as the relationship between humanity and nature, timelessness, and the concept of sacred space.

Film and Other Media

The world of cinema and other visual media like video games also contribute to the perpetuation of stone circles' mystique. Films like "Stonehenge Apocalypse" and games like "The Elder Scrolls" feature stone circles as central elements of their plots or settings, often attributing mystical powers to them. While these interpretations are largely fictional, they resonate with audiences because they draw on a collective curiosity and fascination with these ancient structures. Such depictions, although not always accurate, serve to keep the dialogue about stone circles alive in public imagination, perpetuating both myth and interest.

In summary, stone circles serve as more than just silent relics of the past; they are living entities within our cultural consciousness. Through art and literature, they enter our collective imagination as symbols laden with multiple meanings, from the sacred to the mysterious. Whether captured in the brushstrokes of a Romantic painting, the lines of an epic poem, or the pixels of a modern video game, stone circles continue to inspire and provoke, just as they have for millennia.

CHAPTER 7: FAMOUS STONE CIRCLES

Section 7.1: Stonehenge

Stonehenge is perhaps the most iconic stone circle globally and has piqued human interest for centuries. This prehistoric monument in Wiltshire, England, consists of a ring of standing stones, each roughly 13 feet high, seven feet wide, and weighing approximately 25 tons. But Stonehenge is not merely a spectacle of ancient architecture; it is a complex and multifaceted site that has been the subject of numerous studies, debates, and theories.

Origins and Construction

The construction of Stonehenge was not a singular event but a process that spanned over a millennium, approximately from 3000 BCE to 2000 BCE. It was built in several phases, beginning with a simple circular earthwork enclosure. Later, timber posts were added, eventually replaced by the impressive megaliths we see today. The stones are thought to have been sourced from two main locations: the larger sarsen stones from the Marlborough Downs, about 20 miles away, and the smaller bluestones from the Preseli Hills in Wales, some 150 miles away. The transportation of these stones is still a subject of research and debate, with theories ranging from human and animal power to waterway transportation.

Archaeological Theories

Several theories attempt to decode the purpose behind Stonehenge's construction. Early theories often emphasized its role as a site for religious or ritualistic activities. Druidic ceremonies were often erroneously linked to the site in the 18th and 19th centuries, but modern archaeology has mostly dispelled such associations. More recently, researchers have explored the monument's potential astronomical alignments. Some stones appear to line up with celestial events like the solstices, although the exact purpose behind these alignments remains a subject of debate.

Cultural Significance

Stonehenge is not just an archaeological marvel; it has seeped deep into the fabric of cultural imagination and spirituality. It has appeared in literature, arts, and even in the annals of popular culture, being frequently featured in movies and documentaries. The site has also found its way into New Age spirituality and is a focal point for various neo-pagan celebrations, particularly during the summer solstice.

The place has also generated tourism interest and is a UNESCO World Heritage Site since 1986. The modern challenge lies in balancing tourism and preservation, ensuring that the site retains its structural integrity and mystical allure for future generations.

Scientific Scrutiny

Modern technology has enabled more precise study of Stonehenge. Ground-penetrating radar, laser scanning, and other advanced techniques have unveiled new facets of this ancient structure. For example, evidence of earlier wooden structures and other buried features around the main stone circle have been discovered, offering fresh perspectives on its original purpose and the activities that might have taken place here.

While most scientific investigations have focused on physical attributes and alignments, some studies have even delved into the acoustic properties of the stones. These studies suggest that the placement of the stones could have been designed to produce specific sound effects, possibly contributing to the site's ritualistic aspects.

Summary

Stonehenge remains a timeless enigma, a monument that captures the imagination of researchers, tourists, and spiritual seekers alike. Its complex construction process and the mysteries surrounding its purpose make it a subject of ongoing study. Whether viewed through the lens of archaeology, cultural significance, or scientific scrutiny, Stonehenge offers a multifaceted understanding of how ancient civilizations interacted with their environment and sought meaning in the cosmos.

SECTION 7.2: THE RING OF BRODGAR

The allure of famous stone circles often overshadows some equally fascinating but less-known sites. One such compelling locale is the Ring of Brodgar, situated in the Orkney Islands of Scotland. This chapter delves into the nuances of this often-overlooked but nonetheless historically and culturally significant stone circle.

Background and Location

The Ring of Brodgar is one of the largest and most well-preserved stone circles in Britain. It is part of the Heart of Neolithic Orkney, a group of Neolithic monuments on the Orkney Islands that have been designated a UNESCO World Heritage Site. Located between the Lochs of Stenness and Harray, the circle has a diameter of about 104 meters (341 feet) and originally comprised as many as 60 stones, although only 27 remain standing today. This Neolithic monument is believed to have been erected between 2500 BCE and 2000 BCE.

Architectural Features

The stones used in the Ring of Brodgar are primarily of local sandstone, which varies in height from about 2.1 meters to 4.7 meters. The monument includes a large circular ditch, approximately 3 meters deep and 10 meters wide, encircling the stones. This ditch was likely hewn out of the rock using simple antler picks, a testament to the extraordinary effort that went into its construction. While the precise methods used to erect the stones remain a subject of scholarly debate, it's generally agreed that the builders would have used simple tools and possibly wooden levers to position them.

Ritualistic and Astronomical Significance

Much like other stone circles, the Ring of Brodgar has long been thought to serve ritualistic or religious functions. Excavations in the area have unearthed animal bones and pottery shards, suggesting that the site may have been used for feasts or offerings. Additionally, the circle's layout seems to indicate some astronomical alignment. While no definitive conclusions have been reached, some theories propose that the site could have functioned as an ancient calendar, tracking the cycles of the moon or marking significant solar events like solstices and equinoxes.

Cultural and Folkloric Context

The Ring of Brodgar holds a special place in the folklore and cultural memory of the Orkney Islands. Legends claim that the stones are petrified giants or, alternatively, that they possess healing properties. Local customs, such as the annual tradition of young people walking around the ring to ensure good fortune, speak to the enduring cultural significance of this ancient monument. The site is also an inspiration for artists and writers who have depicted its stark beauty and evocative atmosphere in various forms of media.

Current Status and Preservation

The Ring of Brodgar's status as a UNESCO World Heritage Site aids in its preservation, and it remains an important tourist attraction for the Orkney Islands. While visitor footfall helps raise awareness and generate revenue for conservation, it also poses challenges in terms of wear and tear on the ancient stones. To mitigate this, measures such as sign-posted paths have been implemented to guide visitors around the site without causing undue stress to the monument.

Summary

The Ring of Brodgar stands as an enduring marvel of Neolithic architecture, rich in cultural, ritualistic, and perhaps even astronomical significance. It serves as a reminder that famous stone circles like Stonehenge are just the tip of the iceberg when it comes to understanding these captivating ancient structures. The Ring of Brodgar, with its own unique qualities and cultural traditions, offers an equally intriguing window into the beliefs, technologies, and collective endeavors of ancient societies.

SECTION 7.3: THE SENEGAMBIAN STONE CIRCLES

When the topic of stone circles arises, places like Stonehenge often spring to mind. However, the story of these intriguing formations stretches beyond Europe. One such example is the Senegambian stone circles located in West Africa. This chapter section delves into these lesser-known but equally compelling stone circles, offering a different cultural perspective that enriches our understanding of these ancient wonders.

Historical Context and Discovery

The Senegambian stone circles are primarily located in the countries of Senegal and the Gambia. These circles date back to somewhere between the 3rd century BC and the 16th century AD. Archaeologists believe they served multiple purposes, including religious or ritualistic activities and perhaps even as a form of societal marking. Unlike European circles, which are often built with large, megalithic stones, the Senegambian circles predominantly feature smaller, laterite stones.

Initially, the circles didn't receive much attention from the wider archaeological community. It wasn't until the latter half of the 20th century that concerted efforts were made to study these stone circles, recognizing their significance. As a result, the region containing these circles was designated a UNESCO World Heritage Site in 2006 to help with preservation and further study.

Architectural Characteristics

Architecturally, the Senegambian stone circles are distinct. They usually feature a set of upright stones, averaging around two meters in height, encircling one or more megaliths in the center. Some of these central megaliths also bear carvings that suggest symbolic or ritualistic importance. The stones are primarily made of laterite, a soil type rich in iron and aluminum.

The arrangement of these stones is unique and varies between different circles. Some are lined in a frontal arrangement to face the community, and others seem to be aligned with astral bodies. These varying layouts hint at possible multiple uses or cultural significances that are yet to be fully understood.

Ritualistic and Societal Significance

The Senegambian stone circles are believed to have served ritualistic and societal functions. Excavations have revealed that some circles were associated with burials, supporting the idea that they played a role in rituals concerning life and death. Moreover, objects like pottery, iron tools, and ornaments have been found in and around the circles, adding weight to the theory that these places were sites of community gatherings or societal markers.

Despite ongoing research, much of the circles' original significance remains unclear. Various theories propose that they may have been used in ancestor worship, fertility rituals, or as territorial markers. The presence of trade items and various artifacts also raises questions about the extent of interaction between these societies and their neighbors.

Conservation and Public Engagement

As with other ancient sites, the Senegambian stone circles face challenges related to conservation. Urbanization, agriculture, and other forms of land use have led to the degradation of some sites. However, being a UNESCO World Heritage Site does provide a certain level of protection and international interest, which aids in conservation efforts.

Public engagement programs, such as educational visits and local initiatives, have also been developed to promote awareness and the importance of these circles. Yet, the battle for their preservation is ongoing. It demands a balance between accommodating modern needs and respecting ancient heritage, a struggle faced by many such historical sites around the world.

In summary, the Senegambian stone circles offer a different lens through which we can view the phenomena of stone circles. They introduce a non-European perspective that enriches the overarching narrative, from their unique architectural characteristics to their ritualistic and societal implications. Their existence prompts many questions, serving as a poignant reminder that the story of stone circles is both deep and wide, crossing not just centuries but also continents.

CHAPTER 8: MYSTICAL ASSOCIATIONS

Section 8.1: Druidic Connections

The lore of stone circles often dances along the edge of archaeology, touching upon the mystical, the historical, and the fantastical. One such point of fascination is the rumored link between these stone circles and the Druids. The Druids were high-ranking professionals in various Celtic cultures and were considered religious leaders, legal authorities, medical experts, and holders of lore. Their reputation in history is multifaceted and deeply woven into the cultural tapestry of Britain and other parts of Europe.

The Origin of the Connection

The notion that Druids built or used stone circles is a relatively recent idea, considering the long timeline of both. This concept gained prominence in the 17th and 18th centuries when antiquarians, perhaps overly enchanted by the mystique surrounding both Druids and stone circles, suggested a link between the two. The popularization of this idea can be traced back to figures like John Aubrey and William Stukeley, both of whom were influential in the early study of British antiquities.

Assessing the Validity of the Link

While the Druid-stone circle link is a popular notion, modern scholarship generally dismisses it for several reasons. Firstly, most stone circles predate the period when Druids were active. Many stone circles were erected during the Neolithic period and the early Bronze Age, which stretches back as far as 3000 BCE to 2000 BCE. The Druids, on the other hand, are primarily associated with the Iron Age, which is around 800 BCE to 100 CE in Britain. This temporal misalignment presents a significant hurdle in making a direct connection.

Moreover, there is no concrete archaeological evidence to support this association. While it's true that the Druids may have held ceremonies in natural settings, which could potentially include stone circles, there is no definitive material culture—like artifacts, writings, or carvings—that ties them to these sites. Archaeological surveys have not unearthed any conclusive evidence that could validate this claim.

The Impact of Popular Culture

Despite the lack of empirical evidence, the idea that Druids and stone circles are intrinsically linked persists in popular culture. This is partly because the notion is deeply ingrained in the stories, poems, and artistic works that touch upon Celtic and British folklore. The concept has also been co-opted by modern Druidry, a religious movement that, while inspired by historical Druids, is a largely modern construct. They sometimes use stone circles for ceremonies, thereby perpetuating the perception of an ancient connection.

In the Realm of Possibilities

While it may be tempting to entirely dismiss the connection between Druids and stone circles based on current evidence, it's essential to adopt a nuanced perspective. Some historians and archaeologists allow for the possibility that while the Druids did not construct these stone circles, they could have used them for their ceremonies much later in history. After all, these stone circles were not isolated from cultural developments that happened after their construction. In ancient times, many religious or sacred sites were co-opted and reused by different cultures and belief systems.

The Lesson from the Legend

So, what does this all tell us? While the popular imagination may readily conjure images of Druids conducting mystical rites within the heart of stone circles like Stonehenge, it's important to weigh these romantic notions against factual data. The story of the Druids and stone circles serves as a cautionary tale about how easily fact and fiction can become intertwined, especially when the subject matter lies in the alluring realm of the ancient and mystical. The connection, for now, is more poetic than factual, more a creation of modern narratives than a reflection of ancient realities.

In summary, although the association between Druids and stone circles tantalizes the imagination, there is currently no compelling archaeological evidence to substantiate it. However, it's a topic that continues to enthrall both academic and popular circles, attesting to the enduring allure of these ancient landscapes and the mysteries they hold. The tale of the Druids and stone circles, whether factual or fictional, adds another rich layer to the complex tapestry of cultural, historical, and mystical narratives that surround these enigmatic structures.

SECTION 8.2:
FOLKLORE AND
LEGENDS

Stone circles have long been fertile ground for folklore and legends that span cultures and epochs. These megalithic constructions—often isolated, imposing, and undeniably mystical—have acted as backdrops for tales that range from the mythical to the cautionary. This section delves into the rich tapestry of stories, myths, and legends associated with stone circles, seeking to understand how these narratives shape our perceptions and contribute to the enigmatic aura that surrounds these ancient structures.

The British Isles: Fairies, Giants, and Druids

One cannot discuss the folklore of stone circles without a deep dive into the stories that emanate from the British Isles, home to some of the world's most famous megaliths, such as Stonehenge. In these lands, folklore often attributes the construction of stone circles to magical beings or giants. A recurring theme is that of fairies dancing in circles and turning into stones at dawn. In Cornwall, for instance, the Hurlers, a group of three stone circles, is said to be men turned to stone for playing the ancient game of hurling on a Sunday. In Ireland, some circles are believed to be the meeting places of Druids, where magical and religious rites were performed, although there is scant archaeological evidence to support this.

Scandinavian Lore: Trolls and the Power of Stones

Moving further north to Scandinavia, folklore is also replete with tales of stone circles, often referred to as "judgment circles," where trolls or other supernatural beings are said to meet. A common narrative is that these circles hold the power to heal or provide supernatural abilities. For instance, the stones could be circled a certain number of times to invoke a spell or cure a malady. These stories, while less historically anchored, offer insights into the ancient belief systems that attribute spiritual or magical powers to the very fabric of the Earth.

African Narratives: Ancestors and Spirituality

The Senegambian Stone Circles in West Africa tell a different story, one that is woven into the fabric of ancestral veneration and spirituality. Local legends often describe these megaliths as the work of ancient societies that had a close relationship with the spirit world. Here, stone circles are not just markers of the past; they are active sites for rites and ceremonies that link the living with their ancestors. This dynamic relationship between the physical and spiritual worlds speaks to the universal allure of stone circles as places that transcend time and space.

Modern Adaptations: Cinema and Literature

In modern times, stone circles have been represented in various forms of art and media, amplifying the existing folklore while creating new legends. Films, novels, and TV shows often incorporate stone circles as portals to different dimensions or as focal points for magical events. The notion that a stone circle could be a gateway or hold the power to change one's destiny is a modern elaboration of age-old beliefs, demonstrating how adaptable and enduring these legends are.

The Psychological Aspect: Archetypes and Imagination

The folklore surrounding stone circles can also be viewed through a psychological lens, particularly when examining how these stories resonate with universal archetypes of the human imagination. Whether representing a boundary between worlds, a place of power, or a link to the past, these tales touch upon themes of transformation, duality, and the unknown. The stone circle, in its fundamental form, stands as a mirror to our deepest fears, hopes, and curiosities, making it a symbol that is as powerful in story as it is in stone.

In summary, folklore and legends about stone circles serve as an intertextual layer that deepens our understanding of these enigmatic structures. From tales of magical beings to modern interpretations in media, the narrative landscape surrounding stone circles is as complex and fascinating as the stones themselves. While these stories may not offer empirical evidence or scientific explanations, they fulfill a human need to mythologize and wonder, adding to the ever-expanding narrative that is the secret life of stone circles.

SECTION 8.3: NEW AGE BELIEFS

In a world where technology and science seem to have an answer for almost everything, stone circles serve as humble reminders of the mysteries that still elude us. Many modern belief systems, often categorized under the umbrella term "New Age," have found a deep resonance with these ancient structures. This section delves into the New Age perspectives that enrich the narrative of stone circles, from energy work to spiritual connections.

Sacred Geometry and Stone Circles

In New Age thought, sacred geometry holds that certain shapes and proportions have spiritual significance. Stone circles are often viewed as manifestations of this cosmic geometry. The circle itself is considered a potent symbol, representing unity, wholeness, and the infinite. Those who follow New Age philosophies believe that the geometric layout of the stones can help amplify spiritual energies. By walking a labyrinthine path within these circles, individuals may seek to align themselves with cosmic rhythms, achieving a sense of spiritual balance and enlightenment.

Stone Circles as Energy Hubs

New Age believers often find stone circles to be powerful conduits for spiritual energies. These sites are purported to be vortex points where the Earth's energy is concentrated, enabling those within the circles to tap into this reservoir for spiritual healing or growth. Practices such as Reiki, crystal healing, and shamanic rituals are sometimes conducted within these sites, with practitioners arguing that the stone circles amplify the effectiveness of their practices.

Astrological Significance

Some New Age philosophies also bring astrology into the conversation. The idea that stone circles are aligned with celestial bodies isn't new; it has its roots in archaeological theories as well. However, New Age thinkers often take this a step further, positing that the stone circles can be used for astrological interpretations. By studying the alignment of these circles with celestial bodies, they believe, one may gain insights into the greater cosmic cycles and their impact on human life.

Earth and Elemental Spirits

Stone circles are often thought to be homes or portals for earth spirits and elemental beings in New Age folklore. Elemental spirits, such as fairies, gnomes, and even dragons, are believed to inhabit these sites. Rituals that honor these spirits are not uncommon. For example, offerings of food, crystals, or flowers may be left at stone circles to please the elemental guardians. By doing so, individuals hope to gain their blessings or wisdom.

Channelling and Divination Practices

Another intriguing New Age practice associated with stone circles is channeling. Some individuals claim to receive messages or visions when meditating within these circles. The nature of these messages can range from guidance on personal matters to revelations about universal truths. Similarly, divination practices like tarot reading or rune casting are sometimes carried out within stone circles, again with the belief that the ancient energies within these sites can lend greater clarity or power to these activities.

Criticisms and Counterpoints

It is important to note that New Age beliefs about stone circles are often met with skepticism from the scientific and academic communities. Critics argue that these modern interpretations can be disconnected from the historical and cultural contexts within which these structures were originally built. They caution against attributing anachronistic meanings that could lead to misunderstandings or misrepresentations of these ancient sites. Nonetheless, the New Age perspective offers a lens through which these stone circles are not merely relics of the past but active participants in contemporary spiritual dialogues.

In summary, the New Age perspective offers a rich tapestry of spiritual and mystical associations with stone circles. From the geometry that underscores cosmic truths to the energies believed to course through these sites, stone circles are more than historical or archaeological curiosities to many people today. They are living landscapes imbued with spiritual meanings and potentials that continue to be explored, celebrated, and respected.

CHAPTER 9: TECHNOLOGICAL INSIGHTS

Section 9.1: Remote Sensing and Stone Circles

In a marriage of ancient structures and modern technology, scientists and archaeologists are increasingly employing remote sensing technologies, such as LIDAR (Light Detection and Ranging), to study stone circles. This chapter delves into the fascinating world of how contemporary technologies are opening new vistas in our understanding of these millennia-old structures.

What is Remote Sensing?

Remote sensing refers to the collection of data and information about objects from a distance, typically from aircraft or satellites. Essentially, it allows researchers to scan and map large areas without disturbing the ground. Among the various technologies used in remote sensing, LIDAR has been particularly effective in mapping and studying stone circles. LIDAR sends out laser beams and calculates the time taken for them to return after striking the target object. This information is then processed to create detailed three-dimensional maps.

LIDAR and Stone Circles

The use of LIDAR in the study of stone circles has been groundbreaking. This technology has the ability to penetrate vegetation and soil to some extent, revealing hidden features that are not visible from aerial photographs or even to the naked eye from the ground. This has resulted in the discovery of previously unknown stone circles, as well as more subtle features within known sites. For example, obscured pathways leading to or from the circles, or evidence of surrounding ditches and embankments, have been revealed using LIDAR scans.

LIDAR also plays a crucial role in preserving the integrity of these ancient sites. Traditional excavation methods can be invasive and may compromise the condition of the site. LIDAR scans, however, provide a non-intrusive way to acquire detailed data, thus helping in preservation efforts. Moreover, the data collected can be archived for future studies, serving as a long-term resource for researchers.

Other Remote Sensing Technologies

Though LIDAR stands out for its precision and capability, other remote sensing technologies have also been utilized in the study of stone circles. Infrared photography, for instance, has the ability to reveal variations in vegetation health, which can sometimes indicate the presence of buried stones or archaeological features. Similarly, ground-penetrating radar (GPR) can be useful for studying the subsurface features of these ancient sites.

Collaboration Across Disciplines

One of the fascinating aspects of employing these technologies is that it often leads to collaboration between archaeologists, geologists, environmental scientists, and experts in remote sensing. This multidisciplinary approach not only enriches the quality of the research but also opens up new avenues for interpreting the data. For example, geomorphological insights could provide clues about how the landscape surrounding the stone circles has evolved over time, while botanical studies can suggest what kinds of activities might have taken place there based on the types of plant life that flourish or struggle in the environment.

Ethical Considerations

While remote sensing offers powerful tools for research, it also raises ethical questions concerning data ownership and the commercial exploitation of newly discovered sites. In many cases, stone circles are situated on privately owned or indigenous lands, making the consent and involvement of local communities essential. The data collected may also have cultural or spiritual significance, warranting sensitive handling and interpretation.

Summary

The advent of remote sensing technologies like LIDAR has revolutionized the study of stone circles by providing precise, non-intrusive ways to map and understand these ancient structures. The richness of the data collected not only aids in our understanding of these enigmatic sites but also helps in their preservation. While these technological advances offer promising opportunities for discovery, they also necessitate ethical considerations to ensure responsible research practices. As we continue to employ more advanced technologies in the study of stone circles, one can only anticipate what other fascinating secrets will be unveiled, adding yet more layers to our understanding of these awe-inspiring monuments.

SECTION 9.2:
MATERIAL ANALYSIS

Understanding the stone circles requires more than just observing their shapes, sizes, or orientations. A deeper layer of knowledge comes from studying the very materials that comprise these enigmatic structures. In this vein, material analysis plays an indispensable role. It helps us decode not only the types of stones used but also their possible origins and subsequent alterations, be it by man or nature. This information is vital for formulating theories about the construction techniques, social organization, and even the beliefs of the people who built them.

Petrographic Analysis

One common approach to studying the material composition of stone circles is through petrographic analysis. This involves microscopic examination of thin sections of the stone to understand its mineralogical composition. Petrography can tell us whether the builders used local stone or sourced materials from a distant location. For example, the bluestones at Stonehenge were found to originate from the Preseli Hills in Wales, hundreds of miles away, indicating a well-organized effort to transport them. This discovery altered previous conceptions about the technological capabilities and societal organization of Neolithic communities.

Geochemical Analysis

Geochemical techniques, such as X-ray fluorescence (XRF) and Inductively Coupled Plasma Mass Spectrometry (ICP-MS), provide further insights. These methods allow researchers to identify trace elements in the stones, which can then be matched with potential source locations. The trace elements serve as a sort of fingerprint for the stone, allowing for more accurate sourcing. For instance, by comparing the elemental composition of a stone in a circle with samples from various quarries, researchers can confirm or rule out specific origins.

Radiocarbon Dating of Organic Materials

While stone itself can't be dated using radiocarbon methods, any organic material found in proximity to the stone circle or embedded in the stones can be. For example, remnants of charcoal or plant material found in the soil near the stones could provide clues about the age of the construction. This information is vital in establishing a chronological context for the site and can also corroborate other dating methods like dendrochronology or stratigraphy.

Soil Analysis

Understanding the stone circles is not merely a matter of studying the stones themselves; the surrounding soil can also offer invaluable insights. Through techniques like particle size analysis and pH testing, researchers can gain an understanding of the local environment at the time the stone circle was constructed. For example, a highly acidic soil might suggest that the area was once a bog, providing clues about the landscape and possibly the symbolic importance of the location.

Wear and Erosion Studies

Examining the wear patterns on the stones can offer insights into how they were used or what elements they have been exposed to over the years. Wind and water erosion patterns can indicate the long-term environmental conditions, while specific markings may suggest human interaction, such as carving or chipping. These details, although subtle, can provide hints regarding the circle's functional or ritualistic uses.

In sum, material analysis equips us with essential tools to unravel the intricate details of stone circles. By understanding the types, origins, and alterations of the materials, we can reconstruct aspects of the lives and environments of the people who erected these enigmatic structures. This multifaceted approach —incorporating petrography, geochemistry, radiocarbon dating, soil studies, and wear analysis—ensures a comprehensive understanding that goes beyond mere observation, delving into the very essence of these ancient sites.

SECTION 9.3: DIGITAL RECONSTRUCTIONS

The role of technology in archaeology extends beyond material analysis and remote sensing; it's increasingly encroaching into the realms of experiential research and education. Specifically, the burgeoning fields of computer simulations and virtual reality (VR) have introduced new dimensions to our understanding of stone circles. These digital reconstructions not only allow archaeologists to hypothesize with greater accuracy but also make these ancient structures more accessible to the public.

Simulated Environments and Hypotheses Testing

One of the most powerful applications of computer simulations is their ability to model complex environmental factors. For example, using digitally reconstructed landscapes, researchers can study how sunlight would have interacted with a stone circle at different times of the year. This helps validate or disprove theories regarding the astronomical functions of certain stone circles, a topic often debated in archaeological circles. Similarly, simulated environments can incorporate other elements, like wind patterns and sound waves, to examine whether stone circles had specific ritualistic or symbolic purposes tied to natural phenomena.

The utility of these simulations is often strengthened by

collaboration with experts from other fields, such as astronomy, climatology, and acoustics. Such interdisciplinary research creates a more robust framework for understanding these ancient structures. The outcome is often a set of simulated scenarios that provide a more nuanced understanding of the stone circles' possible original purposes, whether they were ritualistic, calendrical, or something else altogether.

Virtual Reality as a Tool for Education and Public Engagement

Virtual reality has opened up a new frontier in archaeological exploration that can be tapped into by professionals and enthusiasts alike. VR experiences can transport users to a digitized version of a stone circle, complete with the surrounding landscape and any related artifacts. These digital spaces can be extraordinarily detailed, incorporating textures, shadows, and even interactive elements that can be manipulated by the user. This provides an immersive experience, unlike any traditional educational medium, making complex archaeological theories more understandable and engaging for the average person.

Schools and museums are increasingly incorporating VR technology into their curricula and exhibits. These tools not only make the mysterious world of stone circles more accessible but also inspire a new generation of budding archaeologists. Furthermore, virtual tours have been invaluable during periods when physical access to stone circles is restricted, such as during maintenance or conservation projects.

Ethical Considerations and Limitations

As with any form of technology, there are ethical considerations to bear in mind. In the realm of digital reconstructions, questions about accuracy and representation can arise. How faithfully can a computer-generated model recreate the conditions of a site that existed thousands of years ago? Moreover, should these digital models include conjectural elements based on contested theories, and if so, how should these be labeled or otherwise identified to the user? Failure to address these concerns can inadvertently spread misinformation or contribute to the already contested narrative surrounding stone circles.

The issue of accessibility also looms large. While VR technology offers unparalleled immersion, the equipment is costly and not readily available to everyone. In this regard, the technology risks becoming a tool of exclusion, rather than one of broad public education.

Summary

Digital reconstructions through computer simulations and virtual reality offer novel ways to study and experience stone circles. While simulations provide new avenues for hypothesis testing and interdisciplinary research, virtual reality serves as an educational tool that could revolutionize how we engage with archaeological sites. However, both come with ethical considerations that need to be meticulously addressed. As we forge ahead into the digital future, these technologies are poised to become integral elements in the evolving narrative of stone circles, bridging the gap between the ancient and the modern in enlightening ways.

CHAPTER 10: CONTROVERSIES AND DEBUNKING

Section 10.1: Fakes and Forgeries

Stone circles have stirred human imagination for centuries. Their historical significance and, for some, mystical allure have drawn attention from academia, tourists, and spiritual communities alike. Yet, where there is awe and curiosity, there is also an opportunity for deception. Some instances of stone circles have proven to be not as ancient or mystical as initially believed. This section will delve into the topic of fakes and forgeries, aiming to elucidate how, why, and by whom these misleading constructs are made.

Reasons for Creating Fake Stone Circles

One of the driving factors behind the fabrication of stone circles is financial gain. As these sites draw significant interest from tourists and scholars, creating a seemingly ancient stone circle can provide an economic boost to a particular region. In some cases, individuals construct these circles on their land, often with the intent of increasing property value or capitalizing on tourist dollars through guided tours or gift shops.

Another reason for creating fake stone circles is ideological or spiritual. Individuals may construct these circles as part of a modern-day ritual or spiritual path, later claiming them to be ancient in origin to add a layer of authenticity or mystical allure. These practices are often conducted with the intent of aligning the constructed circle with astronomical events or ley lines, claiming a historical and spiritual legacy that doesn't truly exist.

Methods of Fabrication

Creating a believable stone circle is no small feat and requires careful planning and execution. Typically, large stones, resembling the types found at legitimate historical sites, are used. These may be weathered artificially to give them an aged look. Some go the extra mile to use the types of stone that are found in genuinely ancient circles of the region to make the forgery more convincing.

In some cases, fabricated circles have been aligned to mimic the astronomical or geographic features often associated with real stone circles, in an attempt to lend them an air of authenticity. Others go further to inscribe symbols or markings on the stones that may look ancient but are, in fact, modern additions.

Notable Examples

There have been several instances where supposed ancient stone circles turned out to be modern fabrications. One such example is the "Bosnian Stone Circle," initially claimed to be an ancient structure but later proven to be a contemporary creation. Scientific analysis showed the stones were not as old as claimed, and further scrutiny found evidence of modern tools used in their construction.

Another instance is the infamous "Druid's Circle" in Pennsylvania, USA. Initially advertised as an ancient site, it was later revealed to be constructed in the early 20th century as part of a larger garden design. The circle has since been the subject of various articles and studies that have debunked its initial claims of being a legitimate ancient site.

Academic and Public Response

Fakes and forgeries have significant implications, especially in the realm of academia. They can skew our understanding of history, archaeology, and even religious practices. When such a site is debunked, it usually invites a wave of skepticism that can cast a shadow over legitimate historical sites and research. Thus, scholars often employ rigorous methodologies, including radiocarbon dating, petrological analysis, and even LiDAR technology to verify the authenticity of stone circles.

For the general public, the revelation that a stone circle is a fake can be disheartening, especially for those who have visited these sites with a sense of wonder or spiritual aspiration. This underscores the importance of responsible tourism and academic integrity in the exploration and promotion of these ancient structures.

To sum up, while stone circles can offer incredible insights into ancient cultures and belief systems, the field is not without its controversies. Fakes and forgeries exist and have varying motivations behind their creation, from financial gain to ideological fulfillment. Rigorous scientific methods and responsible public engagement are essential for distinguishing the authentic from the fraudulent, ensuring that these fascinating structures continue to be explored and appreciated in their genuine context.

SECTION 10.2: LEGAL AND ETHICAL CONCERNS

Stone circles, often located in remote areas and on private lands, pose intriguing questions about property rights, cultural heritage, and the ethics surrounding their excavation and study. These ancient monuments are replete with historical, spiritual, and sometimes, scientific significance. Therefore, their conservation, study, and public access are topics that inevitably cross into legal and ethical territory.

Land Rights and Ownership

Determining ownership of lands where stone circles are located can be complex. In some countries, these sites might be on private lands, requiring archaeologists and researchers to obtain permissions from landowners to conduct studies. In other cases, the land might be considered public property or might belong to indigenous communities who consider these sites sacred. The conflict between academic interest and property rights has sometimes led to legal disputes.

For instance, in Australia and North America, the struggle over land rights has also been intertwined with indigenous claims and sensitivities. Indigenous communities might regard these sites as ancestral lands and consider the stone circles as integral to their spiritual and cultural heritage. Thus, any excavation or tourist activities could be viewed as infringement or desecration, warranting legal actions to preserve indigenous rights.

Ethics of Excavation

The excavation of stone circles is a subject of ethical debate, particularly when these sites are considered sacred or have cultural importance to local or indigenous communities. While scientific study can yield valuable insights into ancient cultures, the methodologies employed can sometimes be invasive. Therefore, ethical guidelines often stipulate that archaeologists should try non-invasive methods like LIDAR or ground-penetrating radar before resorting to physical excavation.

Moreover, when excavation is deemed necessary, it should ideally be conducted with the consent and, in some cases, the involvement of local communities. This is to ensure that the research is conducted respectfully and that any findings are shared with the community, thereby fostering a sense of collective stewardship and knowledge-sharing.

Tourism and Commercialization

Tourism can be a double-edged sword. While it brings awareness and sometimes much-needed financial resources for preservation, it can also lead to deterioration due to unchecked visitor activities. Additionally, commercialization can sometimes diminish the cultural or spiritual essence of these sites. For example, vendors selling souvenirs close to a sacred site might be seen as a violation of its sanctity.

Legal frameworks often struggle to strike a balance between

making these sites accessible to the public and preserving their integrity. Strict regulations on visitor numbers, guided tours, and educational programs are some ways to manage the impact of tourism. However, the enforcement of such measures often meets resistance from local businesses and other stakeholders, who argue for economic benefits.

International Legislation

Some international frameworks seek to address these concerns, such as the World Heritage Convention, which aims to identify and protect cultural and natural heritage considered to be of outstanding value to humanity. However, these frameworks are often limited by the laws of individual countries and the extent to which they recognize and enforce such international agreements.

Cultural Sensitivity and Public Education

It's essential to approach these sites with cultural sensitivity, especially if they hold religious or ancestral importance. Public education can play a significant role in this, teaching both locals and tourists about the value of these ancient sites, not just as curiosities or attractions but as integral parts of human heritage.

In summary, the legal and ethical concerns surrounding stone circles are complex and multi-layered, often requiring an interdisciplinary approach that combines legal scholarship, ethical guidelines, community engagement, and international cooperation. Navigating these issues respectfully is crucial not only for the advancement of scientific understanding but also for the preservation of cultural integrity and heritage.

SECTION 10.3: PUBLIC MISCONCEPTIONS

In a realm as fascinating and intricate as that of stone circles, misinformation and misconceptions are almost inevitable. The allure these ancient structures possess can easily translate into exaggerated claims, half-truths, or even outright myths. In this section, we aim to correct some of the common misconceptions surrounding stone circles, thereby providing a more nuanced understanding of these captivating landmarks.

Stone Circles as Druidic Temples

One of the most enduring misconceptions is the association of all stone circles with Druidic practices. While it's true that some Druidic groups today use stone circles for their rituals, most of these circles were built long before the period in which Druids are historically documented. Archaeological evidence suggests that the majority of stone circles were constructed during the Neolithic and Bronze Ages, whereas Druids became prominent much later, during the Iron Age.

Astronomical Precision

Another common misconception revolves around the astronomical capabilities of stone circles. While some stone circles like Stonehenge do show remarkable alignments with celestial events, it's a mistake to assume that all stone circles were constructed as ancient observatories. The alignments are often approximate, and many stone circles don't exhibit any significant celestial alignments at all. Moreover, attributing a purely astronomical function diminishes other likely uses for these circles, such as social, ritualistic, or even practical purposes like land demarcation.

Homogeneity in Purpose and Design

The belief that all stone circles were created for a single unified purpose or that they all share similar design elements is misleading. Stone circles vary significantly in their size, design, and the materials used for construction. Their purposes are equally diverse, ranging from social gathering places to sites for ritualistic practices and, in some instances, for astronomical observation. The local geography, culture, and period during which each circle was built contribute to this diversity.

Mystical Energy Fields

The notion that all stone circles are hubs of mystical or supernatural energies is a relatively modern interpretation often linked with New Age beliefs. While it's true that many people report experiencing unusual sensations when visiting these ancient sites, there is yet to be conclusive scientific evidence supporting the existence of energy vortices or ley lines intersecting at stone circles. The sensation of awe or spirituality one might experience could be more closely related to the site's historical gravitas and natural beauty.

Stone Circles as Isolated Phenomena

Many people think of stone circles as isolated historical

phenomena unique to certain cultures or geographies, like the British Isles. However, these structures can be found globally, from the Senegambian Stone Circles in West Africa to the Medicine Wheels in North America. They are not exclusive to any single culture or period but are a recurring architectural motif throughout human history.

In summary, while stone circles continue to fascinate us for many reasons, it's crucial to approach them with a balanced perspective. The aura of mystery surrounding these ancient structures is indeed part of their appeal, but it's equally important to base our understanding on verified information. This avoids the pitfalls of misinformation and allows for a more nuanced and respectful engagement with these enduring landmarks.

CHAPTER 11:
THE FUTURE OF
STONE CIRCLES

Section 11.1: Conservation Efforts

As we approach the concluding chapters of this book, it's essential to acknowledge that stone circles, these ancient markers of time, belief, and culture, are not just relics of the past but a living heritage that we share across generations. While they've withstood the ravages of time and the elements for thousands of years, stone circles now face new challenges that put their existence at risk. This section will delve into the ongoing and future projects aimed at conserving stone circles, ensuring that they continue to enchant and educate future generations.

National and International Initiatives

National governments and international bodies such as UNESCO have taken steps to ensure the preservation of stone circles. Stonehenge, for example, was added to the UNESCO World Heritage Sites list in 1986, providing it with a level of protection and recognition that helps to safeguard its future. Some nations have adopted specific laws designed to protect historical sites, making it illegal to carry out excavations, restorations, or even visitations without proper authorization. Financial grants and academic sponsorships are often provided to support responsible archaeological studies that aim not only to discover but also to preserve.

Community-Based Approaches

Local communities often hold the key to effective conservation strategies. In many instances, they've lived alongside these stone circles for generations and regard them with a blend of reverence and custodial responsibility. Grassroots initiatives can involve everything from organized clean-ups to educational programs in schools, ensuring that the knowledge and respect for these sites are passed down to younger generations. Local tour operators are increasingly trained in responsible tourism, teaching visitors about the cultural and historical significance of these sites while also instructing them on how to engage with the sites in a manner that minimizes wear and tear.

Technological Aids in Conservation

Modern technology has offered new tools for conservation. For example, non-invasive scanning methods like LIDAR (Light Detection and Ranging) allow for detailed mapping of stone circles without disturbing their physical structure. Drones equipped with high-resolution cameras can also monitor the condition of these sites, providing data that can be useful in preventive conservation. The Internet, too, plays a role; digital archives and databases make it easier than ever for researchers around the world to collaborate on preservation methods and share their findings.

Balancing Tourism and Preservation

The allure of stone circles often drives a surge in tourism, which, while beneficial for local economies, can be detrimental to the stone circles themselves. The foot traffic, the occasional urge by tourists to take souvenirs, and even pollution from increased vehicular activity can accelerate the degradation of these ancient sites. Some sites now employ visitor management strategies such as guided tours, restricted access during specific seasons, and interpretive signage to balance educational outreach with conservation. Revenue generated from entry fees often directly funds maintenance and conservation activities.

The Role of Academia and Research

Academic institutions and research organizations play a crucial role in both studying these megalithic structures and ensuring their ongoing conservation. Through rigorous study, often funded by grants aimed at preservation, scholars can deduce the most effective methods for maintaining the integrity of these stone circles. They may also develop materials and technologies specifically designed to protect these ancient stones from the elements while ensuring that any interventions are reversible and minimally invasive.

In summary, the conservation of stone circles is a multifaceted effort involving national and international bodies, local communities, technological innovations, the tourism industry, and the academic world. Each plays a role in ensuring that these awe-inspiring sites remain for future generations to ponder and enjoy. Their future conservation is not just an act of historical preservation but a gift of knowledge and wonder to the generations that follow.

SECTION 11.2: FUTURE RESEARCH AVENUES

As our understanding of stone circles evolves, new research avenues are opening up. This natural progress of knowledge is fueled by technological advancements, interdisciplinary collaborations, and a renewed interest in these ancient structures. As researchers dig deeper, both metaphorically and literally, they are coming up with more questions than answers, which is the hallmark of any vibrant field of study. The quest to understand the origin, purpose, and influence of stone circles continues to yield multiple avenues for future research, some of which we will explore in this section.

Interdisciplinary Approaches

A prevailing trend in recent years is the inclusion of interdisciplinary approaches to studying stone circles. Archaeology remains the cornerstone, but researchers are now collaborating with experts in fields like geology, astronomy, and even computer science. Geological studies can provide insights into the types of materials used and the likely sources of these materials. Astronomical alignments, such as the solstices and equinoxes, also need more rigorous investigation. Given the advanced simulation capabilities we now possess, computer models can help recreate how these circles might have looked or been used in the past, adding depth to our understanding.

Application of Advanced Technologies

Advances in technology provide not just new tools but new ways to think about old questions. Ground-penetrating radar and LIDAR are already being used for topographical mapping, but their full potential has yet to be tapped. Could there be hidden structures or features beneath the surface that offer more context? Isotope analysis could help in tracing the origins of the stones, and thus provide clues to ancient trade or pilgrimage routes. Moreover, with the development and increasing popularity of machine learning and data analytics, researchers can sift through enormous datasets to identify patterns or anomalies that would otherwise go unnoticed.

Unearthing Social and Cultural Contexts

While much has been done to understand the architecture and possible ritualistic or astronomical uses of stone circles, their broader social and cultural contexts are still murky waters. How did these structures fit into the everyday lives of the communities that built them? Were they elite projects or community undertakings? The exploration of artifacts found around these circles, like pottery or tools, could help to reconstruct the social fabric of ancient societies.

Ethnoarchaeology and Oral Traditions

Considering the vast geographical spread of stone circles, integrating local folklore and oral traditions into academic research could be a goldmine of information. Ethnoarchaeology, which bridges ethnography and archaeology, could offer valuable insights. Communities living near these ancient structures often have myths, legends, and historical narratives passed down through generations that could add layers of meaning or offer alternate explanations to established theories.

Climate Change and Its Impact

A somewhat unexplored but increasingly urgent avenue for research is the impact of climate change on stone circle sites. As sea levels rise and weather patterns shift, many of these ancient structures could be at risk. Understanding how climate variables have impacted these sites historically could help in devising strategies for their preservation. Additionally, studies into how these ancient peoples adapted to their changing environments could provide contemporary lessons in sustainability.

In summary, the field of stone circle research is far from static. New methods and theories continually emerge, providing fresh perspectives and unanswered questions. Future avenues for research are as varied as they are promising, fueled by advancements in technology, shifts in disciplinary focus, and the pressing concerns of climate change. The collective endeavor to understand the history, meaning, and future of these enigmatic structures continues to be a multidimensional puzzle that captivates experts and enthusiasts alike.

SECTION 11.3:
STONE CIRCLES IN
THE DIGITAL AGE

The digital age has transformed the way we engage with the world, and stone circles are no exception. From the ways we discover, study, and interact with these ancient sites to how they are represented in digital media, technology has made a profound impact. This section explores the different facets of how the digital age is shaping our relationship with stone circles.

Virtual Visits and Augmented Reality

While the authentic experience of visiting a stone circle can't be wholly replicated, virtual reality (VR) and augmented reality (AR) technologies have created alternatives that are compelling in their own right. With the help of VR headsets, users can virtually walk among the stones of Stonehenge or the Ring of Brodgar from the comfort of their homes. On-site, AR apps can enrich the visitor's experience by overlaying historical data, astronomical alignments, or even recreations of rituals believed to have been conducted at these sites.

Crowdsourced Research and Public Engagement

The digital age has also democratized research to an extent.

While academic research on stone circles remains a specialized field, crowdsourcing efforts have contributed valuable data. For instance, satellite imagery available to the public has enabled the discovery of previously unknown stone circles. Mobile apps allow amateur archaeologists or curious visitors to upload photographs and location data, which could be valuable for ongoing research projects.

Social Media and Online Communities

Stone circles have found new life on platforms like Instagram, where striking images can reach millions and foster greater public interest. Online forums and social media groups also serve as hubs where enthusiasts, academics, and curious individuals can share information, theories, and experiences. These digital communities often serve as the first point of introduction for many people, potentially encouraging physical visits or further academic research.

Digital Archives and Accessibility

Maintaining digital archives has become more crucial than ever for the preservation of knowledge about stone circles. High-resolution 3D scans, detailed topographical maps, and comprehensive databases are now available for many stone circle sites. These digital resources can be valuable for researchers unable to visit the sites in person and also serve as a form of digital preservation, especially important for sites at risk from natural decay or human activity.

Ethical Considerations

While the digital age offers numerous opportunities, it also presents challenges. For instance, the commercialization of VR experiences can raise ethical questions, especially if the revenue is not used for conservation efforts. Additionally, the influx of visitors drawn by digital exposure can stress the ecological balance of these sites. Finally, the digital divide means that these new methods of engagement might be inaccessible for communities that have traditionally been custodians of these sites.

In summary, the digital age has opened new vistas in our interaction with stone circles, making them more accessible and engaging than ever before. Virtual and augmented reality offer new ways to experience these ancient sites, while digital archives preserve invaluable data for future generations. Crowdsourcing and social media have expanded the community of people interested in these megalithic structures, democratizing research and outreach. However, this new frontier of digital interaction also brings with it ethical considerations that require thoughtful attention. Like the stones themselves, our engagement with these ancient circles is complex, multifaceted, and ever-evolving.

CHAPTER 12: CONCLUSION

Section 12.1: Summary of Key Findings

Stone circles, those enigmatic ancient constructions that mystify researchers and captivate the general populace, have proven to be far more than mere clusters of rocks. They are the embodiment of a complex tapestry of historical, cultural, and sometimes even mystical narratives. This book has aimed to shed light on the multifaceted aspects of stone circles, unraveling some of their enigmas while deepening others.

We began with an understanding of what stone circles are—essentially, prehistoric man-made rock formations—and examined their historical context, stretching back thousands of years. Stone circles are not confined to any single geographic area, as many might assume. Indeed, they can be found worldwide, from the British Isles to West Africa, demonstrating the broad appeal and cultural import of these structures across time and space.

Our exploration into the types of stone circles provided an architectural lens through which to understand these ancient landmarks. Some are characterized by recumbent stones, while others feature concentric rings or associated structures like henges. Each design offers clues to the circle's potential purpose and the cultural practices of the people who built them.

Archaeological theories abound when it comes to stone circles. Early 20th-century explanations have given way to more nuanced perspectives, including ritualistic and astronomical interpretations. While many theories posit that stone circles were used for religious or ritualistic purposes, others speculate that these formations functioned as early tools for understanding celestial events.

From an architectural standpoint, the choice of material and construction methods provide more avenues for research. Different stones, from sandstone to granite, were employed in constructing these circles, suggesting diverse local and possibly spiritual considerations. Furthermore, the alignment of many stone circles with natural features like the sun, moon, or other landscape elements implies a deep understanding of spatial orientation.

The book also delved into the esoteric realms of ley lines and energy vortices. These notions, though often sidelined by mainstream archaeology, have captivated those interested in the mystical or spiritual aspects of stone circles. Despite skepticism and scrutiny from the scientific community, these ideas continue to fuel debates and explorations.

Stone circles have not only survived the test of time but have also left an indelible mark on our collective imagination. Their cultural impact manifests in modern religions, art, literature, and even in the realm of tourism. Renowned sites like Stonehenge attract millions of visitors each year, highlighting the continuing allure of these ancient landmarks.

Technological advancements, such as remote sensing and digital reconstructions, have injected new vigor into stone circle research. These tools offer researchers unprecedented ways to study and understand these formations without causing physical damage, thus balancing the need for exploration with preservation.

Despite the volumes of research and interest, stone circles are not without controversies. Issues related to fakes, land rights, and the ethical implications of excavation have muddled the waters. These challenges necessitate cautious and responsible approaches to both study and preservation.

This journey through the world of stone circles reveals that they are far from being settled subjects. The dialogues around them are as dynamic as the structures are static. They continue to provoke questions, inspire theories, and fuel imaginations, ensuring that their allure will remain a constant in an ever-changing world.

SECTION 12.2: UNANSWERED QUESTIONS

While we've examined numerous aspects of stone circles—from their construction and potential uses to their cultural impact and mystical connotations—it's essential to note that many questions remain unanswered. Despite the advances in archaeological research and technology, the true nature, purpose, and scope of stone circles still puzzle researchers and enthusiasts alike. Let's delve into some of the most intriguing questions that remain open for debate.

The Actual Purpose

One of the most obvious questions is, what was the actual purpose of these stone circles? While some theories point to religious or ritualistic uses, others suggest astronomical alignments. Yet, the evidence is often insufficient to conclusively support one view over the other. There's still room for speculation and further study in this area.

Unknown Construction Methods

Despite ongoing research into how stone circles were built, the exact methods remain elusive. Current theories suggest that the stones were moved and erected using a combination of simple machines and human effort. Still, the lack of definitive historical records makes it a topic of continued investigation. Additionally, we don't fully understand how the constructors had the technical skill to align the circles with celestial bodies or natural landmarks precisely.

Cultural Connections

The global distribution of stone circles is also a matter of intrigue. While we've discussed circles predominantly in the United Kingdom and West Africa, they can be found all around the world. Does this wide distribution suggest a universal cultural significance, or could these structures have evolved independently across different societies? Understanding these cultural intersections or divergences could offer a more comprehensive perspective.

Preservation and Sustainability

As these structures age, they are subject to natural deterioration and human interference. The question of how best to preserve them for future generations is a matter of urgency but also an ethical dilemma. Is it right to perform invasive archaeological investigations that may compromise the integrity of these sites? And how should these ancient sites be managed in an era of increasing tourism?

Mystical Associations: Fact or Fiction?

The links between stone circles, ley lines, and energy vortices are subjects of fascination for many but have often been met with skepticism from the scientific community. Can these mystical elements be validated through rigorous scientific analysis? Or will they forever remain in the realm of folklore and speculation?

While numerous queries still float in the academic and public spheres, the questions we've discussed stand out for their complexity and resistance to easy answers. These persistent uncertainties, far from discouraging, actually open up multiple avenues for future research and interpretation. Scholars, amateur enthusiasts, and technological innovators have an extensive field to till as they dig deeper into the myriad mysteries that stone circles continue to present.

In sum, the landscape of stone circle research is far from complete; it's a continually evolving field where each new discovery adjusts our understanding and generates yet more questions. It's this evergreen nature of inquiry that keeps the study of stone circles not just historically relevant but also dynamically aligned with the changing tides of cultural, technological, and scientific developments.

SECTION 12.3: FINAL THOUGHTS

The journey through the world of stone circles is akin to stepping into a vast labyrinth of history, spirituality, science, and art. The intriguing allure of these ancient stones—quietly marking landscapes and time—has clearly spoken to different aspects of human interest, from the rigor of academic disciplines to the fluid realms of spirituality and folklore. It's this unique combination that grants stone circles an almost timeless magnetism, a quality that seems as unyielding as the megaliths themselves.

Throughout this book, we've examined stone circles from multiple perspectives. From the archaeological lenses that zoom into the types of stones used and their specific alignments to the skies, to the sociocultural viewpoints that consider the imprints of these structures on literature, art, and religious practices, we've taken a panoramic view. The fact that modern technologies such as LIDAR and material analysis are being employed alongside studies of ancient legends and spiritual beliefs only adds to the depth of this fascinating subject.

But let's also not forget the ethical and controversial dimensions. As much as we seek to understand, conserve, and celebrate these megalithic configurations, questions about land rights, the legitimacy of some sites, and the boundaries of scientific vs. spiritual interpretations keep the discourse around stone circles vibrant and contentious. The debates serve as a reminder that our interactions with these ancient sites are not mere observations but engagements that have real-world implications.

Of course, one cannot ignore the mystical and speculative angles either. The supposed links to ley lines and energy vortices may not have the empirical backing that some would desire, but they undoubtedly contribute to the aura of mystery that keeps people enthralled. Skeptics and believers coexist in this realm, each offering viewpoints that can either enrich or cloud our understanding, depending on one's perspective. It's an intricate tapestry of narratives that makes the subject so enthralling.

It is not just the stones but the spaces they create—physically, culturally, and conceptually—that draw us in. Whether envisioned as portals to different dimensions, as some New Age theories suggest, or as monuments commemorating communal activities, the empty spaces circumscribed by these megaliths are rich with potential meanings. And so, these stones and the circles they form serve as mirrors reflecting the diversity of human curiosity and interpretation. They remain sites of projective imagination, onto which we cast our theories, beliefs, and sometimes, our deepest desires for connection with something greater than ourselves.

Finally, the resonance of stone circles in the digital age adds another layer to this complex story. Digital reconstructions and virtual reality experiences may offer more people glimpses into the ancient world, but they also raise important questions about authenticity and experience. What is the trade-off when a tactile, sensory engagement with these stones is swapped for a digital interaction? The question is not merely academic but touches on how technology mediates our relationship with history and culture.

In the end, what emerges is that the mystery of stone circles isn't likely to be unraveled entirely, neither by the sharpest of scientific analyses nor the most intuitive of spiritual insights. And perhaps that is where their true allure lies—in their ability to remain elusive, ever inviting us to look closer, think deeper, and wonder more expansively. In this sense, the secret lives of stone circles may well be a reflection of our own enduring quest for understanding in a world brimming with both tangible realities and intangible possibilities.

THE END

Printed in Great Britain
by Amazon